Going Places
Picture-Based English

Book 2

Eric Burton
Lois Maharg

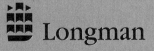
Longman

FOR OUR PARENTS

Going Places: Picture-Based English, Book 2

Consultants:
Barry Bakin, *Van Nuys Community Adult School*
Sally Bates, *Long Beach Unified School District*
Sandee Bergman, *New York City Public Schools Adult Ed.*
Yvonne Nishio, *Evans Adult School*
Susan Rabasco, *San Diego Community College, Mid City Adult Center*
April Rice, *West Hills Community College District*
Michael Rost, *Consultant*

A Publication of World Language Division

Associated companies:
Longman Group Ltd., London
Longman Cheshire Pty., Melbourne
Longman Paul Pty., Auckland
Copp Clark Pitman, Toronto

Acquisitions Director: Joanne Dresner
Acquisitions Editor: Anne Boynton-Trigg
Consulting Editor: Michael Rost
Development Editor: Karen Davy
Project Manager: Helen B. Ambrosio
Text Design: A Good Thing
Cover Design: Joseph DePinho
Text Art: Tonia and Denman Hampson, Baoping Chen, Woodshed Productions
Production: A Good Thing

Library of Congress Cataloging in Publication Data

Burton, Eric
    Going Places: picture-based English/Eric Burton and Lois
Maharg
    p. cm.
  ISBN 0-201-82526-0
  1. English language—Textbooks for foreign speakers. I. Maharg,
Lois. II. Title.
PE1128.B848 1995
428.2 4—dc20   94-49596
                          CIP

7 8 9 10-CRK-03 02 01 00

Contents

	LIFE SKILL AREAS	STRUCTURES
	Following directions Asking questions in class	Imperatives
	Introductions	Formulaic questions
	Requesting help	*To be* Plurals
	Giving instructions	*To be* Prepositions of location
	Giving directions Reading a directory Alphabetizing	Present continuous
	Giving street directions	Present continuous Prepositions of motion
	Using the telephone Alphabetizing	Past of *to be*
	Inquiring about classes	*There is/There are*

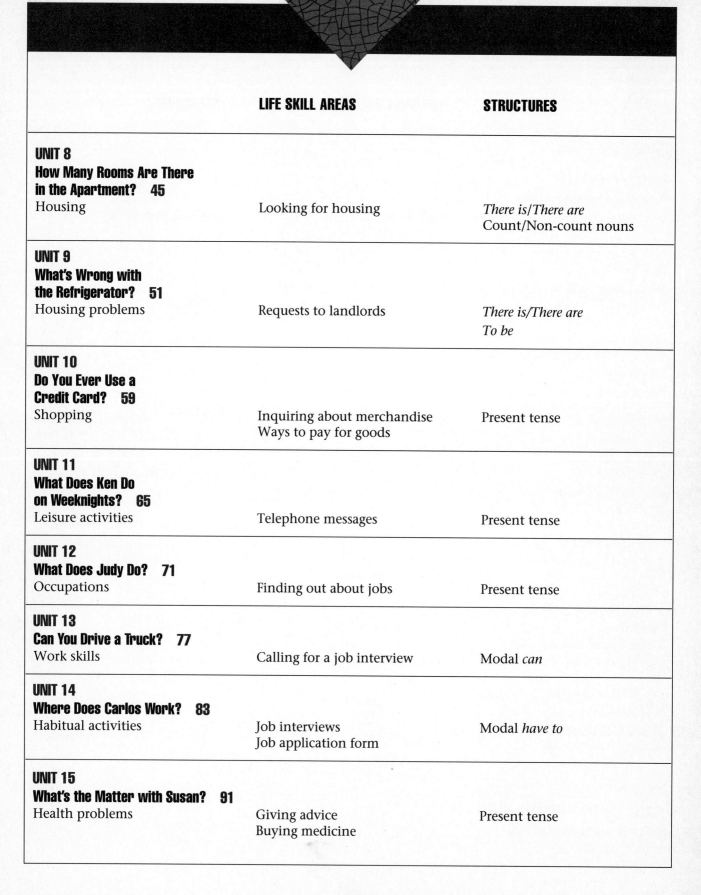

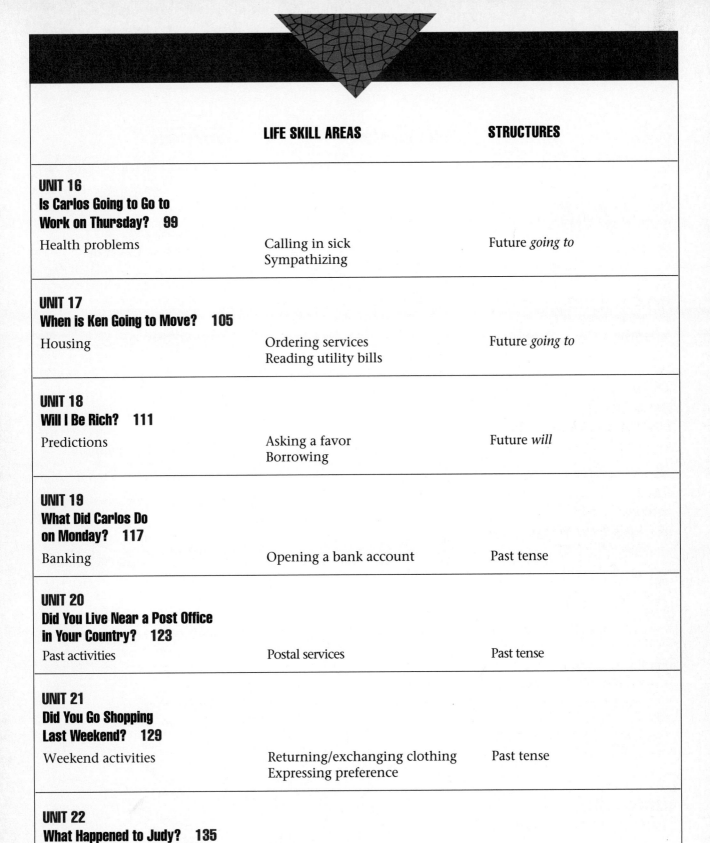

	LIFE SKILL AREAS	STRUCTURES
	Calling in sick Sympathizing	Future *going to*
	Ordering services Reading utility bills	Future *going to*
	Asking a favor Borrowing	Future *will*
	Opening a bank account	Past tense
	Postal services	Past tense
	Returning/exchanging clothing Expressing preference	Past tense
	Calling Emergency 911	Past tense

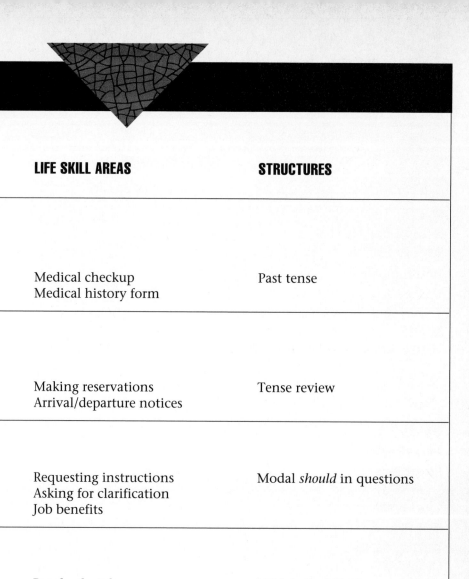

INTRODUCTION

Going Places helps beginning ESL students develop the language they need to carry out everyday activities at work, in the community, and in their personal lives. It

- utilizes uncaptioned pictures as a vehicle for presenting new language and as a springboard for language practice.
- introduces learners to a wide range of practical vocabulary through natural, personalized interaction with the teacher.
- systematically acquaints students with elementary language structures and functional language in such life skill contexts as shopping, work, housing, and health care.
- gives students ample opportunity to utilize the vocabulary and structures they have learned in personalized, meaningful exchanges with their classmates.
- recycles vocabulary and language structures throughout each book and throughout the course.
- provides mutually reinforcing practice in the four skill areas (listening, speaking, reading, and writing), progressing in emphasis from reception to production.
- addresses learners' visual, tactile, and aural learning modalities through a broad range of activities.
- involves students and teachers in conversations that heighten cross-cultural awareness.

Each unit of *Going Places* is taught in three stages:

I) PRESENTATION OF VOCABULARY

1. The teacher presents new vocabulary through personalized, interactive questioning about the pictures on the first page of the unit. (This method of presentation is described in detail on the following pages, and at the beginning of each unit the teacher is referred to specific teaching suggestions for that unit at the back of the book.) During this presentation, the students view the uncaptioned pictures on an overhead transparency (OHT) or in their books.

2. The teacher then directs students' attention to the second page of the unit, where the pictures are reproduced with captions. The students now see the new vocabulary in written form as the teacher reviews and clarifies it, modeling the pronunciation of each item for students to repeat.

3. Students then practice the vocabulary in pairs, one student reading the captions on the second page as the other points to the appropriate uncaptioned picture on the first page. Before the pairwork, the teacher should model this practice with a student, choosing the pictures in random order so students will do the same during the pairwork.

4. Most units include a taped Listen and Write activity to reinforce the new vocabulary aurally and visually. (Tapescripts for these appear in the back of the book.)

5. The conclusion of the vocabulary presentation provides a natural—though not necessary—"breaking off" point for ending a day's lesson, as it gives students a chance to study the new vocabulary at home before proceeding to conversation practice.

II) CONVERSATION PRACTICE

1. The teacher introduces, expands upon, or reviews a key grammatical structure (as it appears in a grammar box) in the context of the new vocabulary.

2. The teacher reads model dialogues in the book that incorporate the new vocabulary and the targeted grammatical structure. Pairs of students then read the same dialogues out loud. Each model dialogue corresponds to a picture on the first page of the unit, which is reproduced beside the dialogue. (Some of the longer dialogues are recorded on the tape, as indicated in the text.)

3. The teacher again directs the students' attention to the uncaptioned pictures on the first page of the unit (on an OHT or in their books). Teacher-student and then student-student pairs model similar dialogues for the class, using various pictures. When pairs of students model the dialogues, the teacher should instruct them to alternate roles (questioner and answerer) with each picture so the class will do the same during pairwork.

4. All the students, practicing in pairs, create similar dialogues based on the uncaptioned pictures. (To jog students' memories, skeletal prompts, which the teacher can write on the chalkboard, are suggested in some units.)

5. Much of the conversation pairwork is personalized, with students exchanging information about each other. After such activities, students should be encouraged to share with the whole class things they learned from their partners. This will reinforce the target language, build familiarity among class members, and help the teacher gauge student mastery of the material.

III) EXPANSION ACTIVITIES

Expansion activities help students achieve life skill competencies through listening, speaking, reading, and writing practice; reinforce the grammar focus of the unit; reinforce and expand the vocabulary of the unit; and further personalize the language students have learned. Expansion activities fall into five categories:

Writing activities—Students write sentences to reinforce and expand on the language they have practiced orally. In most cases, students are instructed to write about themselves and should be encouraged to share one or more of their sentences with the rest of the class.

Listening activities—Students listen to taped conversations and demonstrate comprehension by completing a task (ordering, matching, etc.). In some cases, students then write sentences or create and practice dialogues based on the listening exercises. (Tapescripts for all recorded conversations appear in the back of the book.)

Reading activities—Students read dialogues or stories and demonstrate comprehension by completing a task. In some cases, students then write sentences or create and practice dialogues based on the reading.

Information-gap speaking activities—Students work in pairs, each partner looking at a different page, and ask and answer questions about information on their partner's page.

Culture questions—Students and teacher discuss a question that highlights cultural differences and similarities relating to the topic of the unit.

Note—*Going Places* features **highlighted** formatting of (1) selected vocabulary and expressions appearing *for the first time* in a dialogue or direction line so the teacher can clarify; and (2) salient structural elements so students will take note.

Presenting New Vocabulary with Pictures

On the first page of each unit, teachers are referred to a page in the Teacher's Notes with a list of questions to ask while presenting the pictures on the first page, and an example of how the presentation of the page might start out. Specific teaching notes are also given for selected units. Teachers are urged to read the notes before starting each unit, although with time they may find it unnecessary to refer to the sample presentations. (Additional, more detailed suggestions for carrying out each lesson are provided in the Teacher's Resource Book.)

Below are guidelines for presenting the vocabulary through pictures.

1. The key to successfully presenting the first page of each unit is to create a *natural, personal interaction* between yourself and your students that will keep them continually responding and thus actively engaged.

2. During the presentation, direct students' attention to an OHT of the pictures. If a projector is not available, have students look at the first page of the unit—*not* the second page— in their books. (*You* will be looking at the page in the Teacher's Notes to which you are referred for teaching suggestions.)

3. Build the presentation around simple yes/no and "choice" questions, such as "Do we cook food in the bathroom?" or "Do we wear coats when it's *hot*, or when it's *cold*?"

4. Use words your students are already familiar with and personalize the new vocabulary by relating it to their lives. (See examples, below.) It is not necessary to limit yourself strictly to language that has already been presented in the book, however, since students' receptive abilities are greater than their productive powers.

5. Do not answer your own questions. When necessary, do the following to help students understand and answer your questions:
   a. Use pantomime.
   b. Point to clues in the pictures.
   c. Use "give-away" questions, such as "Is this a *toothbrush*, or a *hammer*?" or "Do we *cook* with a microwave, or *wash clothes* with a microwave?"

d. Simply feed students answers, such as "Who's wearing a shirt in this class? . . . [No answer from students] . . .Well, is Peter wearing a shirt? [touching Peter's shirt] . . . Yes, Peter's wearing a shirt. And who else? . . ."

6. Use each new vocabulary item in several questions as you present it. Also, skip around the page and review frequently to reinforce and check students' retention of items already presented. For example:

"Which picture has the __[bank]__ ?"

"Point to the picture of the __[hammer]__ ."

7. Have students keep their pencils down and notebooks closed during the presentation, to keep their focus on the *oral* interaction. (Reassure them that the new vocabulary is in their books for later reference.) During the presentation, you can write new vocabulary items on the chalkboard as they are introduced *and then erase them after a few moments*. This will give students a "visual take" on the new words, while maintaining the focus on the oral presentation.

8. Adjust the pacing and the length (amount of repetition) of your presentation to your students' abilities and the difficulty of the lesson. A presentation may last between twenty and forty minutes.

9. During the presentation, be concerned primarily that students *understand* the new vocabulary, not that they be able to produce it.

The following examples offer a general idea of what a presentation might sound like:

Picture being presented: a broom (from Unit 2)

Teacher's presentation: Today we're going to talk about things we use at work or at home. What's this picture of? . . . Well, is it a pencil or a broom? . . . Yes, it's a broom. How many parts to a broom? . . . Yes, a broom has two parts [pointing]. How big is a broom? This big? This big? [indicating with hands]? . . . Yes, about this big. Do you have a broom in your house, Dac? . . . You do? Where do you keep your broom? . . . In the kitchen. And what's a broom used for? . . . Yes, it's for sweeping the floor. Where's the floor, everybody? . . . That's right [pointing]. Do you sweep the floor at home, Dac? . . . Oh, what a good husband! Marco, what color is the broom in your house? You don't know? My goodness, I'd hate to see the floor in your house! . . . Oh, I see. Your wife does the sweeping. Well, OK then . . .

Picture being presented: department store (from Unit 4)

Teacher's presentation: Today we're going to talk about stores. Look at this picture. What kind of store is this? . . . Well, where do you buy clothes? . . . Yes, at a department store. What are some department stores in town? . . . Yes, Macy's . . . And Woolworth's. Those are both department stores . . . That's right, Mei, you can also buy other things at department stores. Do you live near a department store, Thuy? . . . You live near Woolworth's? What about you, Angela? Is there a department store near your house? . . . There isn't. Now, back to our picture. Who's at the department store? . . . Yes, Judy is. And what's she doing there? . . . Well, is she buying food? . . . No. She's buying clothes.

English for the Classroom

1. Look at the pictures. Read the sentences. Repeat them after your teacher.

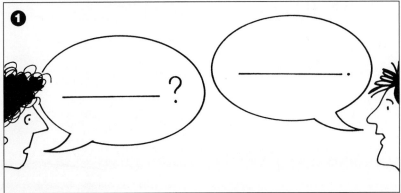

Ask the question.   **Answer.**

Write the words.

Write the sentence.

Repeat.

Continue. (Go on.) (Next.)

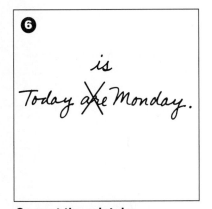

Correct the mistake.

Study.

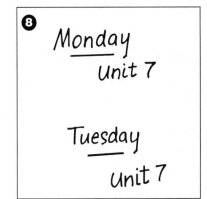

Review.

Topic: the classroom
Life skills: following directions;
asking questions in class
Structure: imperatives

1

2. Write the number of the sentence under the correct picture.

1. Continue.
2. Review.
3. Correct the mistake.
4. Write the words.
5. Answer.
6. Repeat.
7. Study.
8. Ask the question.
9. Write the sentence.

4

_____

_____

_____

_____

_____

_____

_____

_____

Teacher, see page 199 for follow-up activities.

3. Look at the pictures. Read the words and sentences. Repeat them after your teacher.

❶ small

What does this mean?
(What is the meaning?)

❷ small

How do you pronounce this?
(What is the pronunciation?)

❸ small

What is the opposite?

❹ small

s-m-a-l-l

How do you spell this?
(What is the spelling?)

❺

small	big
dime	house
tooth	China
mouse	elephant

Give examples.

❻

A. big

B. hap-py

C. con-tin-ue

A. one syllable
B. two syllables
C. three syllables

❼

A. book

B. books

A. singular
B. plural

❽

A. ABCDEFGHIJKLMNOPQRSTUVWXYZ

B. AEIOU

C. BCDFGHJKLMNPQRSTVWXYZ

A. 26 letters in the alphabet
B. 5 vowels
C. 21 consonants

4. Match the questions and answers.

LITTLE

1. What is the first consonant?

2. What is the first vowel?

3. Give an example.

4. What does it mean?

HAPPY

5. How do you pronounce it?

6. How do you spell it?

7. What is the opposite?

8. How many syllables?

STUDENT

9. Singular or plural?

STUDENTS

10. Singular or plural?

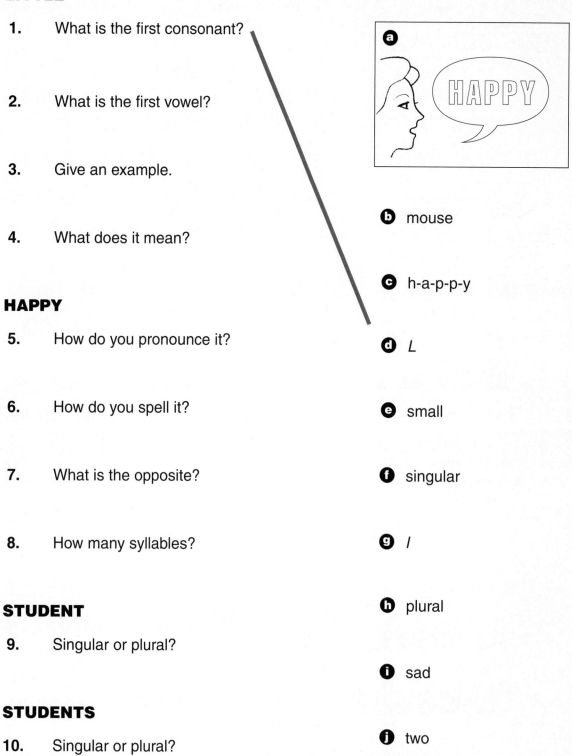

a HAPPY

b mouse

c h-a-p-p-y

d *L*

e small

f singular

g *I*

h plural

i sad

j two

Teacher, see page 199 for follow-up activities.

Introductions

Ken Wong and Judy Johnson are **coworkers** at the Ace Bicycle Factory.

Ken is Judy's boyfriend.

Susan Gomez is a new employee at the factory.

Mr. Sato is their boss.

Introductions

At Home

This is Susan and her husband, Carlos.

They have two children—Linda and Paul.

They have two pets—a cat and a parrot.

What's Your Name?

1. Look at the pictures. Answer your teacher's questions. (Teacher, see page 200.)

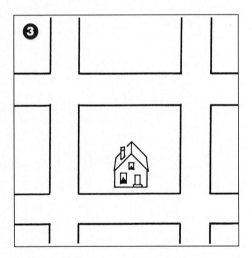

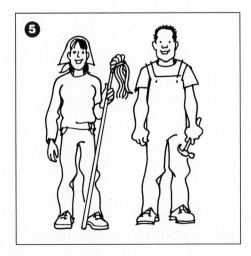

Topic: **personal information**
Life skill: **introductions**
Structure: **formulaic questions**

Getting to Know People

2. Listen to the questions. Repeat them after your teacher.

①
What's your name?

②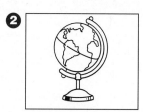
Where are you from?

③
Where do you live?

④
Are you married?
Do you have children?

⑤
What do you do?

⑥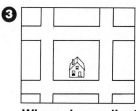
What do you do on weekends?

Listen and Write

3. Listen and complete the sentences.

1. I have two sons. Do you have __children_____?

2. On weekends, I go shopping. What do you do on _____?

3. I'm from Mexico. Where are you _____?

4. I work in a store. What _____ _____ do?

5. Are you single or _____?

6. I live downtown. Where do you _____?

7. Hi. I'm Susan. What's your _____?

8. What do _____ _____ on Saturdays and Sundays?

Conversation

4. PAIRWORK. Look at page 7. Ask and answer questions with a partner.

5. Susan is a new employee at the Ace Bicycle Factory. Listen to Mr. Sato introduce her to Judy. Then practice the conversation with your teacher.

Mr. Sato: Judy, this is Susan Gomez. She's our new office **manager.**

Judy: Hi, Susan. Nice to meet you.

Susan: Nice to meet you too, Judy. What do you do here at the bicycle factory?

Judy: I'm the secretary.

Susan: Oh, that's nice.

6. Listen to Mr. Sato introduce Susan to other employees at the bicycle factory. Circle the picture of the question Susan asks.

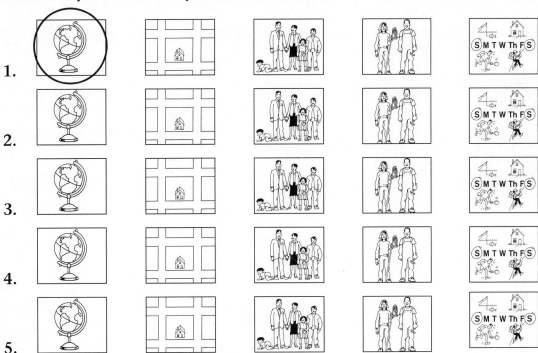

Listen again. Complete the answers to Susan's questions.

1. (Tran) I'm from ___Vietnam._____

2. (Ivan) I fix _____

3. (Lisa) Yes. I have _____

4. (Tom) I live on _____

5. (Ken) I go dancing with my _____

7. Susan is introducing herself to Mrs. Sato. Listen to the conversation. Then practice it with your teacher and with a partner.

Susan: Hello. I'm Susan Gomez. What's your name?
Mrs. Sato: I'm Mrs. Sato.
Susan: Nice to meet you, Mrs. Sato.
Mrs. Sato: Nice to meet you too, Susan.
What do you do?
Susan: I'm the new office manager.
How about you?
Mrs. Sato: I'm a **housewife**.
Susan: I see. Do you have children?
Mrs. Sato: Yes. We have four.
Susan: Oh, that's nice.

8. Choose a new partner and introduce yourself. Ask and answer questions. Write your partner's answers on the lines.

1. _____

2. _____

3. _____

4. _____

5. _____

6. _____

9. Introduce your partner to the class. Tell the class your partner's name and two more things about him or her.

Example: This is Eva Lopez.
She's from Mexico.
She's married, and she has three children.

How do people greet each other in your country?

What's That? What's It For?

1. Look at the pictures. Answer your teacher's questions. (Teacher, see page 200.)

1

2

3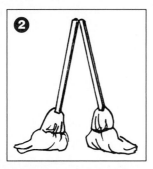

4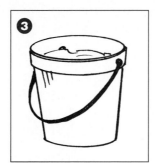

5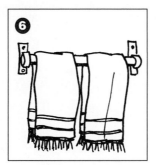

6

7

8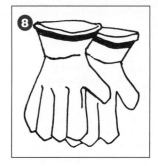

9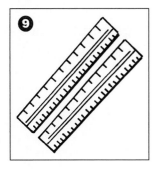

10

11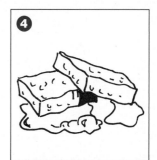

12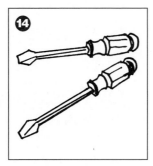

13

14

15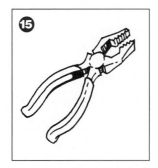

16

Topic: useful objects
Life skill: requesting help
Structures: *to be*; plurals

11

Things We Use

2. Learn the new words. Listen to the words. Repeat them after your teacher.

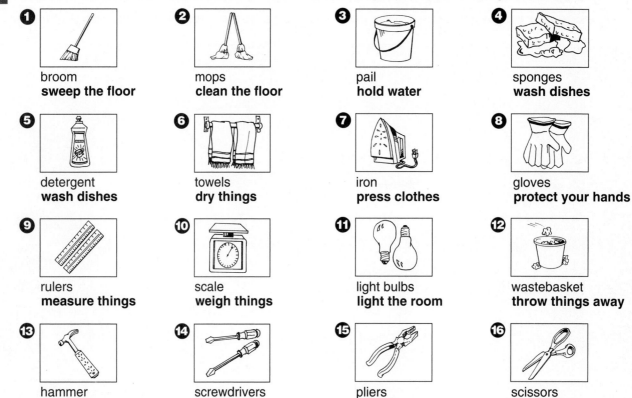

1 broom
sweep the floor

2 mops
clean the floor

3 pail
hold water

4 sponges
wash dishes

5 detergent
wash dishes

6 towels
dry things

7 iron
press clothes

8 gloves
protect your hands

9 rulers
measure things

10 scale
weigh things

11 light bulbs
light the room

12 wastebasket
throw things away

13 hammer
fix things

14 screwdrivers
fix things

15 pliers
fix things

16 scissors
cut things

PAIRWORK. Practice with a partner. Student A, look at this page and say the words. Student B, look at page 11 and point to the pictures.

Listen and Write

3. Listen and complete the sentences.

1. I need to clean the floor. Can you give me the _____?

2. I want to dry the dishes. Where's the _____ ?

3. You can throw that away in the _____ over there.

4. I always protect my hands with _____ when I work.

5. I need to cut this paper. Where are the _____ ?

6. I want to measure this desk. Can you give me that _____, please?

7. I need to weigh this letter. Do you have a _____ ?

Conversation

What's that?	**It's a** _____ .
What are those?	**They're** _____ .

What's it for?	_____ **ing.**
What are they for?	

 4. Listen to the conversation. Then practice it with your teacher.

A: Excuse me.
B: Mmm-hmm?
A: Can you tell me…
  What's that?
B: It's a scale.
A: What's it for?
B: Weighing things.

A: And what are those?
B: They're pliers.
A: What are they for?
B: Fixing things.
A: Thanks a lot.
B: Don't mention it.

PAIRWORK. Now look at page 11. Make new conversations with a partner.

Plurals

5. Read the **rules** and **examples** with your teacher.

Singular	Plural	
book car	books cars	Add -s.
box dish lunch bus	boxes dishes lunches buses	Add -es.
baby ⟵ consonant	babies	Drop the **y.** Add -**ies.**
boy ⟵ vowel	boys	Add -**s.**
life shelf	lives shelves	Change **f** to **v.**
person child man woman foot tooth	people children men women feet teeth	**irregular** words

Write the plurals.

1. brother _____

2. person _____

3. day _____

4. dish _____

5. foot _____

6. apple _____

7. lady _____

8. shelf _____

9. book _____

10. class _____

11. fork _____

12. lunch _____

13. stamp _____

14. woman _____

15. watch _____

16. glass _____

17. house _____

18. box _____

19. half _____

20. man _____

21. child _____

Now say the words with your teacher and classmates.

Asking for Help at Work

6. Learn the new words. Look at the pictures and repeat the words after your teacher.

closet

cabinet

drawer

Listen to the conversations and practice them with your teacher.

Ruth: Where's the mop?
Ken: It's in the closet.
Ruth: In the closet?
Ken: Yes.
Ruth: Can you please bring it to me?
Ken: Sure. No problem.
Ruth: Thanks.

Ivan: Where are the pliers?
Ken: They're in the drawer.
Ivan: In the drawer?
Ken: Yes.
Ivan: Can you please bring them to me?
Ken: Sorry, but I'm **busy** now.
Ivan: OK.

7. Ken's coworkers are asking for things. Listen to the conversations. Circle the correct location. If Ken helps, circle *yes*. If Ken can't help, circle *no*.

1. closet (cabinet) drawer | (yes) no

2. closet cabinet drawer | yes no

3. closet cabinet drawer | yes no

4. closet cabinet drawer | yes no

5. closet cabinet drawer | yes no

8. Look at the picture and complete the conversation. Then practice it with a partner.

Judy: Where's the _____?

Ken: It's in the _____ .

Judy: In the _____?

Ken: Yes.

Judy: ____ ____ _____bring it to me?

Ken: Sure. No problem.

Judy: Thanks.

9. You are asking a coworker for help at work. Complete the conversations. Then practice them with your partner.

1. **You:**   Where _____?

   Coworker: _____ .

   You: In the _____?

   Coworker: Yes.

   You: Can you please _____?

   Coworker: Sure. No problem.

   You: _____ .

2. **You:**   Where _____?

   Coworker: _____ .

   You: _____?

   Coworker: Yes.

   You: _____?

   Coworker: Sorry, but I'm busy now.

   You: _____ .

In your country, do men and women do the same kinds of jobs?

Where's the Pail?

1. Look at the picture. Answer your teacher's questions. (Teacher, see page 200.)

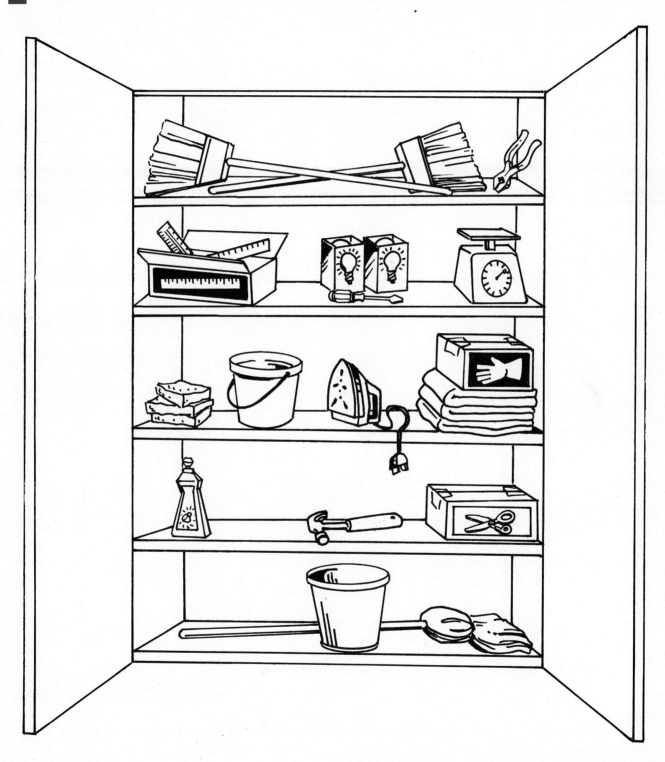

Topic: **shelf locations**
Life skill: **giving instructions**
Structures: *to be;* **prepositions of location**

17

Shelf Locations

2. **Read the sentences. Repeat them after your teacher.**

1. The pail is **to the right of** the sponges.
   The sponges are **to the left of** the pail.
   or The pail is **next to** the sponges.

2. The gloves are on **the far right.**
   The sponges are on **the far left.**

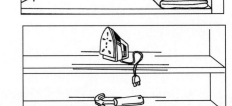

3. The gloves are **on top of** the towels.

4. The iron is | **over** | the hammer.
           | **above** |

5. The hammer is | **under** | the iron.
           | **below** |
           | **beneath** |

6. The mop is **behind** the wastebasket.

7. The brooms are on the **top** shelf.

8. The mop is on the **bottom** shelf.

9. The scale is on the second shelf **from the top.**

10. The scissors are on the second shelf
    from the bottom.

11. The sponges are on **the middle shelf.**

12. The hammer is in **the middle of the shelf.**

PAIRWORK. Practice with a partner. Student A, look at this page and say the sentences. Student B, look at page 17 and point to the picture.

Listen and Write

3. Listen and complete the sentences.

1. The scale is on the second _____ .

2. The sponges are on the middle shelf, on the_____ _____ .

3. The mop is_____ the wastebasket.

4. The hammer is in the _____ _____ _____ shelf.

5. The pail is _____ _____ _____ _____ the iron.

6. The gloves are _____ _____ _____ the towels.

7. The wastebasket is on the _____ shelf.

8. The scissors are_____ the towels.

Conversation

4. Listen to the conversation. Then practice it with your teacher.

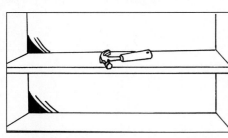

A: Excuse me. Can you help me?
B: Sure. What is it?
A: Where's the mop?
B: On the bottom shelf, behind the wastebasket.

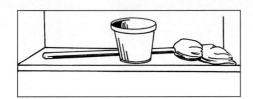

A: Oh, yeah. I see it. And where are the pliers?
B: On the top shelf, on the far right.

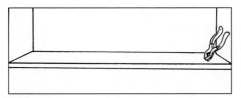

A: Oh, yeah. And how about the hammer?
B: On the second shelf from the bottom,
   in the middle of the shelf.
A: Oh, right. Thanks a lot!

PAIRWORK. Now look at page 17. Make new conversations with a partner.

Following Instructions at Work

5. Ken's **supervisor** is giving him instructions. Listen to the conversation.
Then practice it with your teacher.

Supervisor:	Ken?
Ken:	Yes?
Supervisor:	Please put this screwdriver in the cabinet.
Ken:	Sure. On which shelf?
Supervisor:	On the top shelf, on the far right.
Ken:	Top shelf, far right. **Got it.**

6. Listen to six more conversations between Ken and his supervisor.
Draw a line from each thing to the correct location in the cabinet.

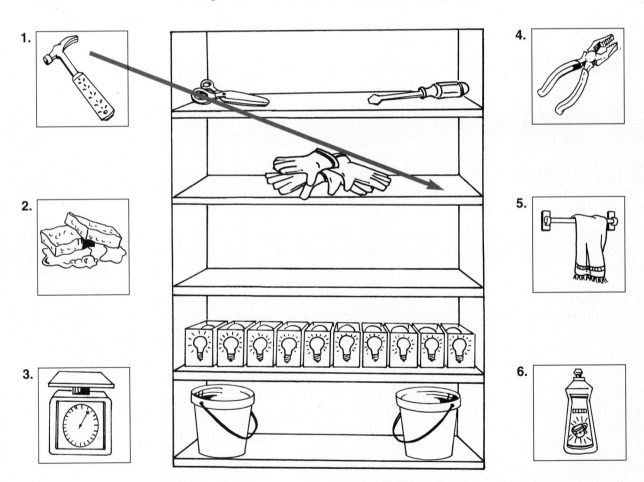

 In your country, do people spend time with their supervisor or boss after work?

Giving and Following Instructions

INFORMATION GAP. Work with a partner. Student A, look at this page. Student B, look at page 22.

7. Student A, you are the supervisor. Student B is the worker. The worker doesn't know where to put the things in the cabinet. Tell the worker where to put them.

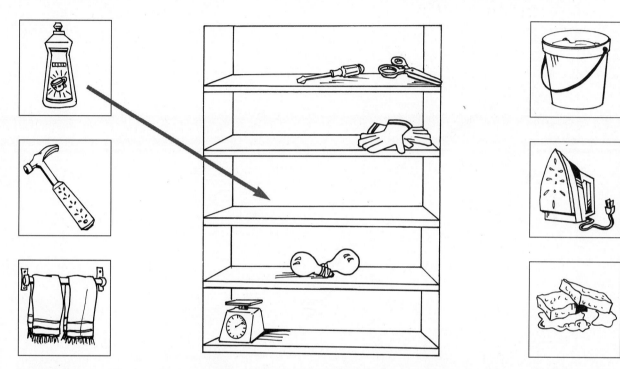

Now you are the worker and Student B is the supervisor. Listen as the supervisor tells you where to put the things above. Draw a line to the correct location on the shelves.

8. Where are the detergent, the hammer, the towels, the pail, the iron, and the sponges? Write complete sentences.

1. ___The detergent is on the middle shelf, on the far left.___

2. _____

3. _____

4. _____

5. _____

6. _____

Giving and Following Instructions

INFORMATION GAP. Work with a partner. Student B, look at this page. Student A, look at page 21.

7. Student B, you are the worker. Student A is the supervisor. Listen as the supervisor tells you where to put the things below. Draw a line to the correct location on the shelves.

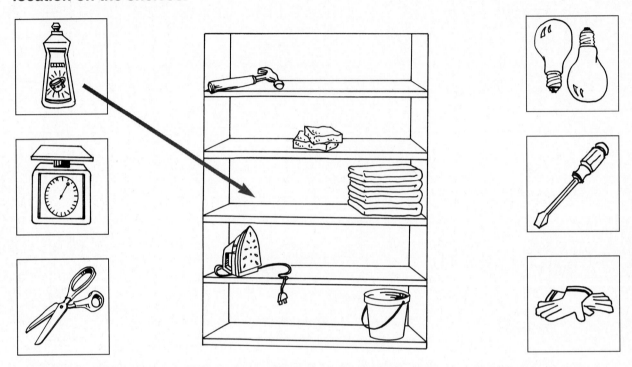

Now you are the supervisor and Student A is the worker. The worker doesn't know where to put the things in the cabinet. Tell the worker where to put them.

8. Where are the detergent, the scale, the scissors, the light bulbs, the screwdriver, and the gloves? Write complete sentences.

1. _The detergent is on the middle shelf, on the far left._

2. _____

3. _____

4. _____

5. _____

6. _____

Where's Judy?
What's She Doing?

1. Look at the pictures. Answer your teacher's questions. (Teacher, see page 201.)

Judy

Susan and Carlos

Ken

Mr. and Mrs. Sato

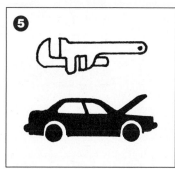

Ivan

Paul and Linda

Ruth

Andy and Marco

Tran

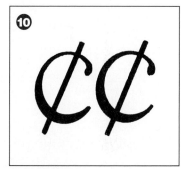

Lisa and Joe

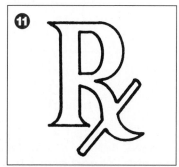

Tom and Marsha

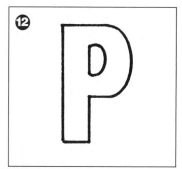

Kathy

Topic: stores and merchandise
Life skill: giving directions
Structure: present continuous

23

Businesses

2. Learn the new words. Listen to the words. Repeat them after your teacher.

❶ department store
buy clothes

❷ bakery
buy bread and cake

❸ hardware store
buy tools

❹ grocery store (supermarket)
buy food

❺ auto repair shop
get the car fixed

❻ barber shop *or* beauty salon
get a haircut

❼ bank
get cash

❽ furniture store
buy furniture

❾ toy store
buy toys

❿ thrift shop (secondhand store)
buy used things

⓫ drugstore (pharmacy)
buy medicine

⓬ parking lot
park the car

PAIRWORK. Practice with a partner. Student A, look at this page and say the words. Student B, look at page 23 and point to the pictures.

Conversation

What's	he she	_____ing?	He's She's	_____ing.
What **are** they			They're	

3. Practice the conversation with your teacher.

A: Where's Judy?
B: At the department store.
A: What's she doing there?
B: She's buying clothes.

A: What about Susan and Carlos? Where are they?
B: At the bakery.
A: What are they doing there?
B: They're buying bread and cake.

PAIRWORK. Now look at page 23. Make new conversations with a partner.

Writing Practice

4. Write about where your family members are now and what they are doing.

Examples: My brother is at home. He's watching television.

My children are at the park. They're playing with their friends.

1. _____

2. _____

3. _____

4. _____

5. _____

6. _____

At a Shopping Center

5. Learn the new words. Look at the pictures and repeat the words after your teacher.

shoe store

card shop

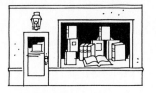
bookstore

candy shop

Judy is at a shopping center. Listen to her conversation. Then practice it with your teacher.

Judy: Excuse me. I'm looking for a bookstore.
Clerk: Go to the second floor.
ABC Bookstore is down the hall to the left.
Judy: Second floor, to the left. Thank you.

6. Repeat the names of the stores after your teacher. Then listen to the conversations. Circle the correct floor. Then circle *left* or *right*.

	Which floor?					Which side?	
1. Sue's Candy Shop	1st	2nd	(3rd)	4th	5th	left	(right)
2. Toy World	1st	2nd	3rd	4th	5th	left	right
3. Guy's Shoe Store	1st	2nd	3rd	4th	5th	left	right
4. Eva's Bakery	1st	2nd	3rd	4th	5th	left	right
5. Cute Cards	1st	2nd	3rd	4th	5th	left	right
6. Betsy's Beauty Salon	1st	2nd	3rd	4th	5th	left	right

7. Here are the stores at City Shopping Center. Repeat the names of the stores after your teacher.

Cute Cards	Joe's Groceries	Sue's Candy Shop
Low-Cost Drugs	Eva's Bakery	Fine Furniture
ABC Bookstore	Guy's Shoe Store	Betsy's Beauty Salon
Toy World	May's Department Store	Dad's Hardware

Here is the City Shopping Center directory. Write the names of the missing stores. Put them in **alphabetical order**.

CITY SHOPPING CENTER
DIRECTORY

Store	Floor
ABC Bookstore	2
Betsy's Beauty Salon	5
_____	4
_____	1
_____	2
_____	3
_____	4
_____	1
Low-Cost Drugs	1
_____	1
_____	3
_____	5

Practice the conversation with your teacher.

A: Where is ABC Bookstore?
B: It's on the second floor.

PAIRWORK. Make new conversations with a partner about all of the stores at City Shopping Center.

Shopping Near Your Home

8. Write the names of the stores near your home.

_____
(grocery store)

_____
(drugstore)

_____
(department store)

_____
(bookstore)

_____
(hardware store)

_____
(bakery)

_____
(furniture store)

_____
(beauty salon)

_____
(shoe store)

_____
(toy store)

_____
(candy shop)

_____
(card shop)

Now write the names of the stores in alphabetical order.

1. _____

7. _____

2. _____

8. _____

3. _____

9. _____

4. _____

10. _____

5. _____

11. _____

6. _____

12. _____

 Are there shopping centers in your country?

Where's Susan Going?

1. Look at the pictures. Answer your teacher's questions. (Teacher, see page 201.)

1 Susan

2 Ken and Judy

3 Carlos

4 Mr. and Mrs. Sato

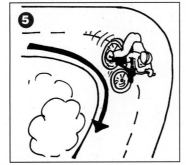

5 Ivan

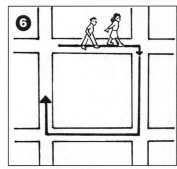

6 Paul and Linda

7 Tom and Marsha

8 Tran

9 Andy and Marco

10 Lisa and Joe

11 Ruth

12 Kathy

Topic: getting around town
Life skill: giving street directions
Structures: present continuous; prepositions of motion

29

Prepositions of Motion

2. Learn the new words. Listen to the words. Repeat them after your teacher.

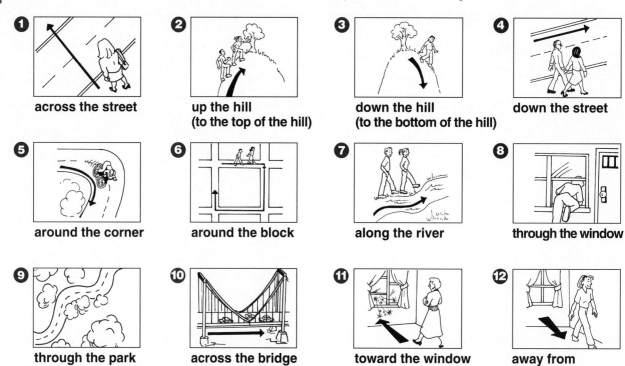

1. across the street

2. up the hill
(to the top of the hill)

3. down the hill
(to the bottom of the hill)

4. down the street

5. around the corner

6. around the block

7. along the river

8. through the window

9. through the park

10. across the bridge

11. toward the window

12. away from
the window

PAIRWORK. Practice with a partner. Student A, look at this page and say the words. Student B, look at page 29 and point to the pictures.

Listen and Write

3. Listen and complete the sentences.

1. Mr. and Mrs. Sato are walking _____ _____ _____ .

2. Tran is going _____ the window.

3. Lisa and Joe are going _____ the bridge.

4. Paul and Linda are walking _____ _____ _____ .

5. Carlos is walking _____ _____ _____ of the hill.

6. Ruth is walking _____ the window.

7. Ken and Judy are going _____ _____ _____ of the hill.

8. Kathy is walking _____ _____ the window.

Conversation

Where's	he she	going?
Where **are** they		

Why **is**	he she	going there?
Why **are** they		

4. Practice the conversations with your teacher.

A: Where's Carlos going?
B: Down the hill.
A: Why is he going down the hill?
B: Because he's going home.

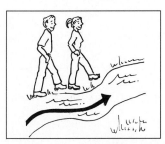

A: Where are Tom and Marsha walking?
B: Along the river.
A: Why are they walking along the river?
B: Because they're going fishing.

PAIRWORK. Now look at page 29. Make new conversations with a partner. Make up your own answers for *Why?*

Street Directions

5. Judy is asking for directions. Listen to her conversation. Then practice it with your teacher.

Judy: Excuse me. I'm looking for May's Department Store.
Is it near here?
Man: Yes, it is. Go down the street two blocks.
Judy: Two blocks?
Man: Yes. Then turn right on 4th Street.
Judy: Right on 4th?
Man: Yes. Then go down the hill. May's Department Store is
at the bottom of the hill on your right.
Judy: Thank you.

Street Directions

6. Listen to the conversations. Draw a line from the store to the correct location on the map.

1. Fine Furniture

2. Toy World

3. Low-Cost Drugs

4. Betsy's Beauty Salon

5. ABC Bookstore

6. Dad's Hardware

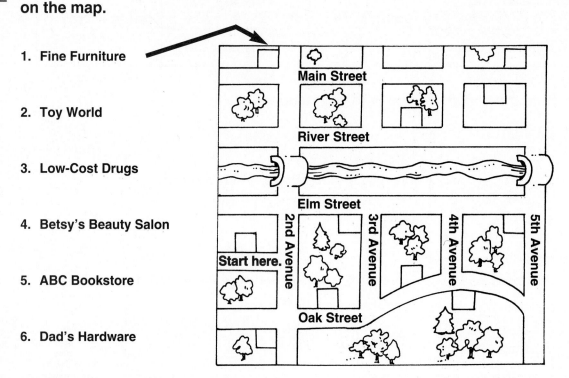

Main Street
River Street
Elm Street
Oak Street
2nd Avenue
3rd Avenue
4th Avenue
5th Avenue
Start here.

7. Read the example. Then write directions from school to your home. Tell them to a partner.

Example: Go out the front door and turn left. Go down the street two blocks. Then turn right on Mason Street. Go one block and turn left. My house is the third house on the left.

_____

_____

_____

_____

_____

 Are there street signs in your country? How do people give directions?

Where Was Carlos during the Earthquake?

1. Yesterday there was a big earthquake at 2:47 P.M. Look at the pictures of where everyone was. Answer your teacher's questions. (Teacher, see page 201.)

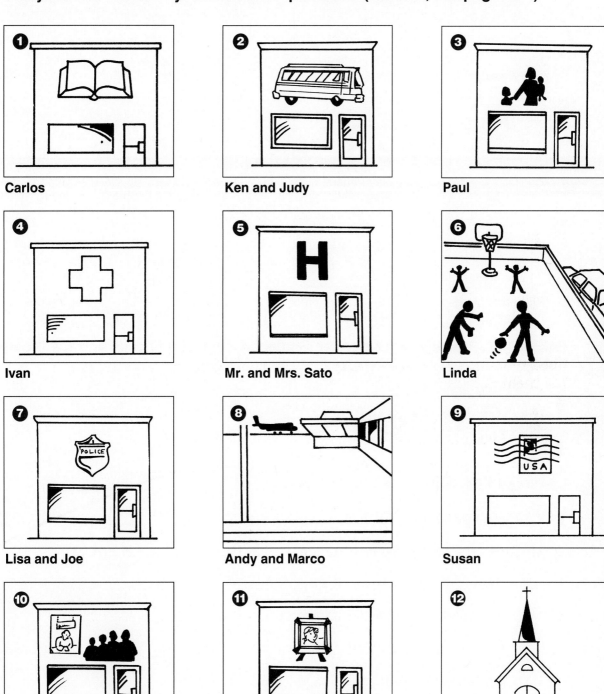

❶ Carlos

❷ Ken and Judy

❸ Paul

❹ Ivan

❺ Mr. and Mrs. Sato

❻ Linda

❼ Lisa and Joe

❽ Andy and Marco

❾ Susan

❿ Ruth

⓫ Tom and Marsha

⓬ Tran

Topic: community resources
Life skill: using the telephone
Structure: past of *to be*

Community Resources

2. Learn the new words. Listen to the words. Repeat them after your teacher.

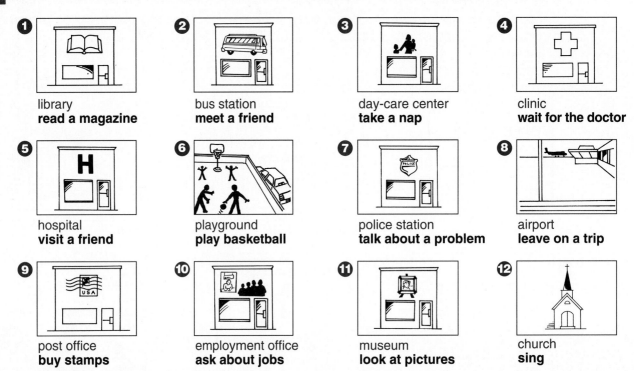

① library
read a magazine

② bus station
meet a friend

③ day-care center
take a nap

④ clinic
wait for the doctor

⑤ hospital
visit a friend

⑥ playground
play basketball

⑦ police station
talk about a problem

⑧ airport
leave on a trip

⑨ post office
buy stamps

⑩ employment office
ask about jobs

⑪ museum
look at pictures

⑫ church
sing

PAIRWORK. Practice with a partner. Student A, look at this page and say the words. Student B, look at page 33 and point to the pictures.

Listen and Write

3. Listen and complete the sentences.

1. Paul was taking a nap at the _____ _____ .

2. Mr. and Mrs. Sato were visiting a friend at the _____ .

3. Susan was buying stamps at the _____ _____ .

4. Tom and Marsha were looking at pictures at the _____ .

5. Ken and Judy were meeting a friend at the _____ _____ .

6. Tran was singing a song in _____ .

7. Ruth was asking about work at the _____ office.

8. Lisa and Joe were talking about a problem at the _____ _____ .

Opening and Closing Times

4. Listen to the telephone conversations and write the opening and closing times.

A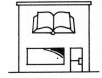

opens _____

closes _____

B

opens _____

closes _____

C

opens _8:00_____

closes _5:00_____

D

opens _____

closes _____

E

opens _____

closes _____

F

opens _____

closes _____

Conversation

Where	**was**	he? she?	
	were they?		

What	**was**	he she	doing?
	were they		

5. Listen to the conversation. Then practice it with your teacher.

Ken: That was a terrible earthquake yesterday!
Susan: It sure was! I was really **scared**.

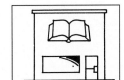

Ken: Where was Carlos at the time?
Susan: At the library.
Ken: What was he doing there?
Susan: Reading a magazine.

Ken: Where were Mr. and Mrs. Sato?
Susan: At the hospital.
Ken: What were they doing there?
Susan: Visiting a friend.

PAIRWORK. Now look at page 33. Make new conversations with a partner.

Learn about Your Classmates

Where were you _____?	What were you doing?

6. Practice the conversation with your teacher.

A: Where were you at seven o'clock last night?
B: At home.
A: What were you doing?
B: Eating dinner.

A: Where were you five years ago?
B: In Vietnam.
A: What were you doing?
B: Going to school.

PAIRWORK. Now close your book and make new conversations with a partner.

Writing Practice

At _____	I he she	was	_____ ing.
	we they	were	

7. Write sentences about you and your family or friends yesterday.

Examples: <u>At 7:00 A.M. I was sleeping at home.</u>

<u>At 9:00 A.M. my children were studying at school.</u>

1. _____

2. _____

3. _____

4. _____

5. _____

8. Repeat the names of the **branch** libraries after your teacher.

Children's Library	Bank Street Library	Downtown Library
Daly City Library	East Bay Library	Booker Library
Center Street Library	Adams Library	Allen Library
English Library	Business Library	First Street Library

Here is a page from a telephone directory. Write the names of the missing libraries. Put them in alphabetical order.

Branch Libraries

Adams Library	1205 Main St	583-9573
_____	89 2nd Ave	367-4870
_____	604 Bank St	583-5072
_____	1790 Green St	367-4901
_____	17 5th Ave	367-0486
_____	916 Center St	583-7758
_____	18604 Riverside	367-8376
_____	1357 Silver St	583-9515
_____	100 Main St	583-2900
_____	308 12th Ave	583-1847
_____	2246 Fine St	367-8862
First Street Library	1566 1st St	367-3883

Practice the conversation with your teacher.

A: What's the address of Adams Library?
B: 1205 Main Street.
A: What's the telephone number?
B: 583-9573.

PAIRWORK. Make new conversations about the libraries with a partner.

9. Look in your telephone directory for a library near your home. Write the name, address, and telephone number.

Name: _____

Address: _____

Telephone number: _____

Directory Assistance

10. Look at the map. Repeat the names of the cities after your teacher.

11. Listen to Susan on the telephone. Then practice the conversation with your teacher.

Operator: Operator. What city, please?
Susan: Los Angeles.
Operator: Go ahead.
Susan: Can you tell me the number for Happy Day-Care Center?
Operator: The number is 964-1207.

12. Listen to the conversations. Write the name of the city and the telephone number. Then practice the conversations with a partner.

1. **Operator:** Operator. What city, please?

   Les: _____ .

   Operator: Go ahead.

   Les: Can you tell me the number for the Bank Street Health Clinic?

   Operator: The number is _____ .

2. **Operator:** Operator. What city, please?

   Sally: _____ .

   Operator: Go ahead.

   Sally: Can you tell me the number for the employment office?

   Operator: The number is _____ .

3. **Operator:** Operator. What city, please?

   Tony: _____ .

   Operator: Go ahead.

   Tony: Can you tell me the number for Mercy Hospital?

   Operator: The number is _____ .

Do working people leave their children at day-care centers in your country?

UNIT 7

Is There a Listening Lab at Our School?

1. Look at the pictures. Answer your teacher's questions. (Teacher, see page 202.)

Topic: school facilities
Life skill: inquiring about classes
Structure: *there is/there are*

39

2. Learn the new words. Listen to the words. Repeat them after your teacher.

1 listening lab	**2** typing classes	**3** library	**4** computers
5 counselors' office	**6** tape recorders	**7** copy machine	**8** night classes
9 student lounge	**10** vending machines	**11** bookstore	**12** emergency exit

PAIRWORK. Practice with a partner. Student A, look at this page and say the words. Student B, look at page 39 and point to the pictures.

Listen and Write

3. Listen and complete the sentences.

1. Can you please tell me where the _____ is?

2. Excuse me. What time do _____ _____ start at this school?

3. Pardon me. Is there a _____ _____ at this school?

4. Could you please tell me where the _____ is?

5. I have a question. Are there any _____ classes at this school?

6. Excuse me. Which way is the counselors' _____ ?

7. Pardon me. Are there any _____ at this school?

8. Excuse me. How can I get to the _____ _____ , please?

Conversation

| **Is** there a _____ in _____ ? | Yes, there is.
No, there isn't. |
| **Are** there **(any)** _____ in _____ ? | Yes, there are.
No, there aren't. |

4. Practice the conversations with your teacher.

A: Is there a library at our school?
B: Yes, there is.
A: Where is it?
B: On the second floor.

A: Are there any vending machines at our school?
B: Yes, there are.
A: Where are they?
B: Downstairs.

A: Is there a student lounge at our school?
B: No, there isn't.

PAIRWORK. Now look at page 39. Make new conversations with a partner.

Writing Practice

5. Does your school have these things? Check (✔) *Yes* or *No*.
If you check *Yes*, write where.

	Yes	No	Where
restrooms	✔		*on the floor*
library			
computers			
counselors' office			
copy machine			
listening lab			
emergency exits			

6. **Practice the conversations with your teacher.**

A: Is there a department store in your **neighborhood**?
B: Yes, there is.
A: How far is it from your house?
B: About a five-minute walk.

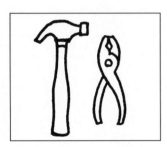

A: Is there a bank in your neighborhood?
B: Yes, there is.
A: How far is it from your house?
B: Three blocks.

A: Is there a toy store in your neighborhood?
B: Yes, there is.
A: How far is it from your house?
B: Just a few minutes by bus.

A: Is there a hardware store in your neighborhood?
B: No, there isn't.

How far?

A ten-minute walk.
A five-minute drive.
Fifteen minutes by bus.
Three blocks.

PAIRWORK. Now look at page 23. Make new conversations with a partner.
Ask: 1. *Is there?* 2. *How far?*

Writing Practice

There's a		
There are	**some**	
	many	
	two/three/four . . .	_____ in my neighborhood.
There aren't **any**		
There are no		

7. Write sentences about your neighborhood.

Examples: There's a day-care center in my neighborhood.

There aren't any trees in my neighborhood.

1. _____

2. _____

3. _____

4. _____

5. _____

6. _____

Calling about Classes

 8. When you call for information, sometimes there is a **recorded message**. Listen to the messages about classes. Then read them with your teacher.

1. Hello. This is The Learning School. For information about **kindergarten** classes, press *one*. For information about grades one to five, press *two*. For information about grades six to eight, press *three*.

2. At The Learning School, there are kindergarten classes in the morning and in the afternoon. To **enroll** your son or daughter, come to the main office and get a **registration form**.

Calling about Classes

9. Repeat the names of the classes after your teacher. Then listen to the messages. Write the correct telephone key. Then circle when the classes are and where to go for a registration form.

Classes	Telephone key	When?			What office?	
1. typing	3	morning	(afternoon)	(night)	(main)	counselors'
2. ESL		morning	afternoon	night	main	counselors'
3. computer		morning	afternoon	night	main	counselors'
4. kindergarten		morning	afternoon	night	main	counselors'
5. citizenship		morning	afternoon	night	main	counselors'
6. drivers' education		morning	afternoon	night	main	counselors'

Conversation

10. Practice the conversation with your teacher.

A: Are there any typing classes at your school?
B: Yes, there are.
A: When are they?
B: In the morning and at night.

A: Are there any kindergarten classes at your school?
B: No, there aren't.

Talk about other classes with your teacher. **List** the classes below. Then make new conversations with a partner.

1. _cooking_   3. _____   5. _____

2. _____   4. _____   6. _____

Are there schools for adults in your country?

How Many Rooms Are There in the Apartment?

1. Look at the pictures. Answer your teacher's questions. (Teacher, see page 202.)

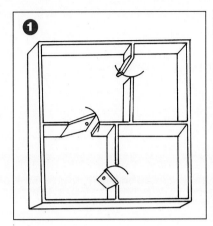

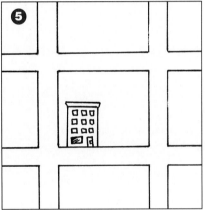

Topic: housing
Life skill: looking for housing
Structure: *there is/there are;*
count and non-count nouns

45

Looking for an Apartment

2. Read the questions. Repeat them after your teacher.

 1. How many rooms are there in the apartment?

 2. Is the apartment furnished or unfurnished?

 3. Is there parking?

 4. Is there a washer and dryer?
(Are there laundry facilities?)

 5. What's the location of the apartment?

 6. How much is the rent?

 7. Who pays utilities?

 8. How much is the deposit?

 9. How long is the lease for?

Utilities
gas
electricity
water
garbage collection

PAIRWORK. Practice with a partner. Student A, look at this page and say the questions. Student B, look at page 45 and point to the pictures.

Conversation

3. Ken is looking for an apartment.
He sees this **sign** in the window of a house.

> FOR RENT
> 1 bedroom apt.
> 293-6548

Later Ken calls the **manager.** Listen to the conversation. Then practice it with your teacher.

Ken: Hello. I'm calling about the apartment for rent. How much is the rent?
Manager: $640 a month.

Ken: I see. Who pays utilities?
Manager: The **landlord.**

Ken: Mm-hmm. And is there parking?
Manager: Yes, there is. But parking is **extra.**
Ken: When can I see it?
Manager: Any time before five o'clock today.

PAIRWORK. Now look at page 45. Make new conversations with a partner. **Take turns** asking questions and being the manager. The manager can give any answer.

Finding Out about Places for Rent

4. Do you know what these **abbreviations** mean? Talk about them with a partner. Then ask your teacher. Write the words on the lines.

1. BR _____
2. W/D _____
3. lg. _____
4. sm. _____
5. nr. bus _____
6. util. incl. _____
7. yd. _____

8. new cpt. _____
9. avail. 3/1 _____
10. pkg. _____
11. $250 dep. _____
12. 1st/last _____
13. eves. _____
14. nites _____

5. You can find out about places for rent in For Rent ads. Read the ads with a partner. Ask your teacher if you don't understand. Then write answers to the questions.

HOUSES	APARTMENTS FURNISHED	APARTMENTS UNFURNISHED
$925 Richmond. Sm. 2BR, furnished, util. incl. 775-3856 nites.	$525 Mission. 2BR, new cpt., 1st/last. Avail. 10/1. 682-8309 eves.	$750 Downtown. Lg. 1BR, W/D, pkg. avail., $400 dep. 885-3856 days.
$1150 Bayview. Lg. 2BR 2 bath, sm. yd., nr. bus. 624-8993	$600 Westwood. 1BR, W/D, nr. bus, no pets. 336-9006 nites.	$875 2 BR nr. Mason Park. New cpt., util incl., avail. 1/15. 772-8570 days.
$1200 Sunset. 3BR, lg. yd., W/D, new cpt., garage. 987-6554 eves.	$1095 Lg. 2BR, 1st and Baker. W/D, view, sm. yd. 326-8572.	$1275 Ocean View. 2BR, W/D, view. 1st/last. 982-8885 nites.

1. Is there an apartment downtown? ___Yes, there is.___

    Is it furnished or unfurnished? ___It's unfurnished.___

2. Is there a three-bedroom house? _____

    Are there laundry facilities there? _____

3. What's the location of the $600 apartment? _____

    Is it near the bus? _____

4. When is the apartment near Mason Park available? _____

    When can you call? _____

5. Is there an apartment with a yard? _____

    Where is it? _____

6. Is the house in Richmond large? _____

    How much is the rent? _____

    Are utilities included? _____

7. How much is the rent for the Ocean View apartment? _____

    How much is the deposit? _____

 How do people find housing in your country?

Count and Non-count Nouns

6. **Count nouns** have a singular and a plural. Look at these examples of count nouns. Answer your teacher's questions. (Teacher, see page 202.)

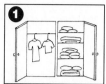

closets

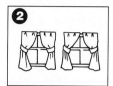

windows

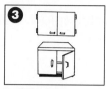

cabinets

trees

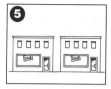

stores

Non-count nouns are always singular. Look at these examples of non-count nouns. Answer your teacher's questions.

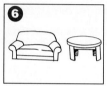

furniture

traffic

noise

crime

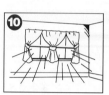

light

Conversation

COUNT	**Are** there **many** _____ in _____ ?	Yes, there are. No, there aren't.
NON-COUNT	**Is** there **much** _____ in _____ ?	Yes, there is. No, there isn't.

7. Listen to the conversation. Then practice it with a partner.

 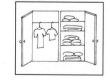 

Ken: Is there much light in the apartment?

Manager: Yes, there is.

Ken: Good. Are there many closets in the apartment?

Manager: No, there aren't.

Ken: I see. Well, are there many trees in the neighborhood?

Manager: Yes, there are.

Ken: That's good. Is there much traffic in the neighborhood?

Manager: No, there isn't.

Is there much Are there many	_____ in your	home? neighborhood?

8. PAIRWORK. Look at the pictures below. Ask a partner about his or her home and neighborhood.

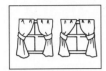   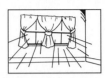 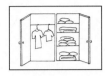

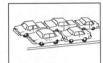    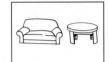

Writing Practice

Count		Non-count	
There are a lot of There aren't many There aren't any	_____ in _____ .	There's a lot of There isn't much There isn't any	_____ in _____ .

9. Write about your home and your neighborhood.

Examples: <u>There's a lot of light in my apartment.</u>

<u>There aren't many trees in my neighborhood.</u>

1. _____

2. _____

3. _____

4. _____

5. _____

More Non-count Nouns							
coffee	tea	food	salt	money	trouble	fog	snow
milk	water	meat	sugar	music	work	rain	wind
oil		rice		time			

What's Wrong with the Refrigerator?

1. Look at the pictures. Answer your teacher's questions. (Teacher, see page 202.)

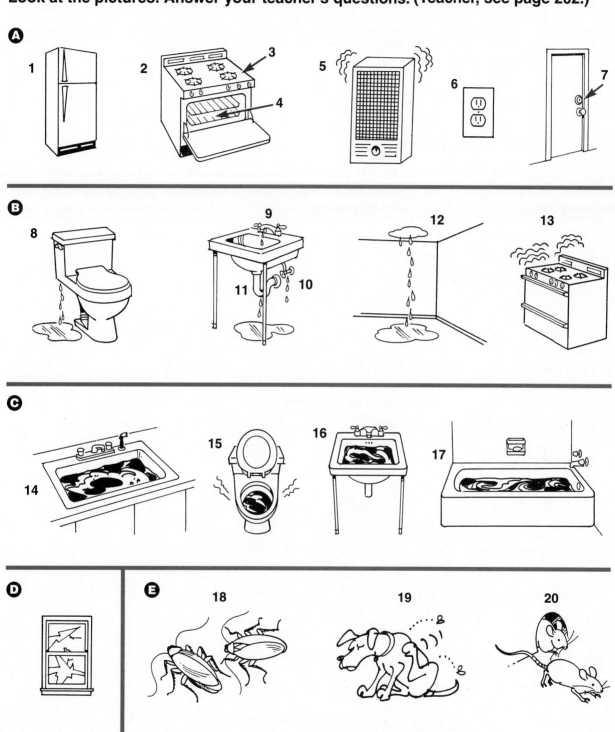

Ⓐ 1 2 3 4 5 6 7

Ⓑ 8 9 10 11 12 13

Ⓒ 14 15 16 17

Ⓓ

Ⓔ 18 19 20

Topic: **housing problems**
Life skill: **requests to landlords**
Structures: *there is/there are; to be*

Apartment Problems

2. Learn the new words. Listen to the sentences. Repeat them after your teacher.

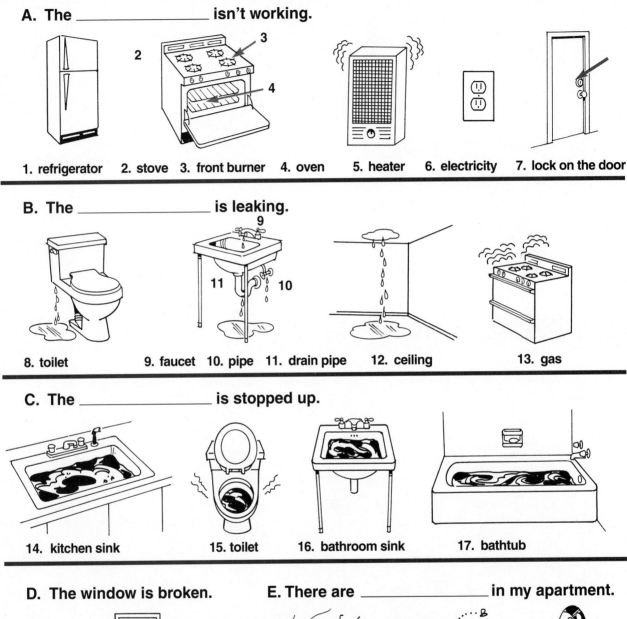

A. The _____ isn't working.

1. refrigerator   2. stove   3. front burner   4. oven   5. heater   6. electricity   7. lock on the door

B. The _____ is leaking.

8. toilet   9. faucet   10. pipe   11. drain pipe   12. ceiling   13. gas

C. The _____ is stopped up.

14. kitchen sink   15. toilet   16. bathroom sink   17. bathtub

D. The window is broken.

E. There are _____ in my apartment.

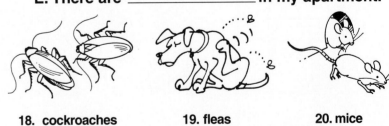

18. cockroaches   19. fleas   20. mice

PAIRWORK. Practice with a partner. Student A, look at this page and say the sentences. Student B, look at page 51 and point to the pictures.

Listen and Write

3. Listen and write the number of each conversation under the correct picture.

A

B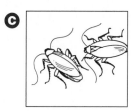

C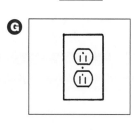

D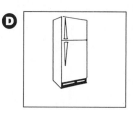

_____

_____

_____

_____

E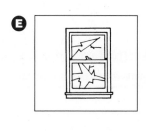

F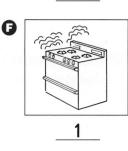

G

H

_____

1

_____

_____

Conversation

4. Listen to the conversations. Then practice them with your teacher.

Tenant:	There's a problem in my apartment.
Landlord:	What's wrong?
Tenant:	The refrigerator isn't working.
Landlord:	I'll take care of it.
Tenant:	Thank you.

Tenant:	There's a problem in my house.
Landlord:	What's wrong?
Tenant:	There are cockroaches in the kitchen.
Landlord:	I'll take care of it.
Tenant:	Thank you.

PAIRWORK. Now look at page 51. Make new conversations with a partner. Take turns being the tenant and the landlord.

What's Wrong with the Refrigerator? 53

5. Listen to the telephone conversation. Then practice it with a partner.

A: Hello, Mr. Jones?

B: Speaking.

A: Mr. Jones, this is Ruth Ames, your tenant in number three.

B: Oh, hello, Ms. Ames.

A: There's a problem in my apartment. The bedroom window is broken.

B: It is?

A: Yes. **Would you please** look at it today?

B: Sure. I can **stop by** at five o'clock. Is that OK?

A: That's fine. See you then.

Look at the pictures and complete the conversation. Then practice it with your partner.

A: Hello, Mr. Hill?

B: Speaking.

A: Mr. Hill, this is Tom Brown, _____.

B: Oh, hello, Mr. Brown.

A: _____.

_____.

B: It is?

A: Yes. _____ look at it today?

B: Sure. _____. Is that OK?

A: That's fine. _____.

Do most people in your country rent, or do they have their own homes?

What's Wrong with This Kitchen?

6. Look at the picture. Answer your teacher's questions. (Teacher, see page 203.)

Safety at Home

7. Learn the new words. Listen to the sentences. Repeat them after your teacher.

1 There's poison on the table.

2 The window is cracked.

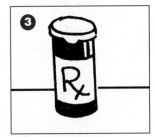

3 There's medicine on the table.

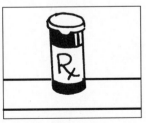

4 There are too many plugs.

5 There's garbage on the floor.

6 The electric cord is hanging down.

Conversation

8. Practice the conversations with your teacher.

A: There's medicine on the table in this kitchen.
B: I know. That's not **safe**.
A: How about *your* kitchen?
B: No way! There isn't any medicine in *my* kitchen.

A: The window in this kitchen is cracked.
B: I know. That's **dangerous**.
A: How about *your* kitchen?
B: No way! The window in *my* kitchen isn't cracked.

PAIRWORK. Now look at page 55. Make new conversations with a partner.

Problems at Home

9. Listen to the conversation. Then practice it with your teacher.

Susan: Hi, Ken.

Ken: Hi, Susan. How are you?

Susan: I'm fine. How about you?

Ken: Not so good. There are cockroaches in my kitchen!

Susan: Oh, no! Call your apartment manager.

Ken: He isn't home today.

Susan: Then write a **note** and **leave** it in his mailbox.

Ken: Oh, that's a good idea. Thanks.

Now read Ken's note to the manager.

10/25

Dear Mr. White:
There's a problem in my apartment. There are cockroaches in the kitchen. Would you please call me or stop by today? My number is 555-9830.
Thank you.

Ken Wong
Apartment #19

Problems at Home

10. Tell a partner about a problem in your home. Then write a conversation about your problem and practice it with your partner.

A: Hi, _____ .

B: Hi, _____ . How are you?

A: I'm _____ . How about you?

B: Not so good. _____

_____ .

A: Oh, no! Call your _____ .

B: _____ isn't home today.

A: _____ .

B: Oh, that's a good idea. Thanks.

Now write a note to your manager or landlord.

Dear _____ :

      There's a problem _____

_____

_____

_____

_____

UNIT 10

Do You Ever Use a Credit Card?

1. Look at the pictures. Answer your teacher's questions. (Teacher, see page 203.)

  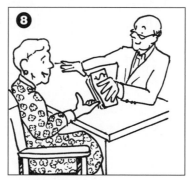

 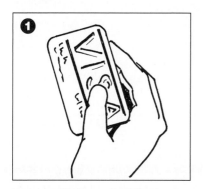 

Topic: shopping
Life skill: inquiring about merchandise
Structure: present tense

2. Learn the new words. Listen to the words. Repeat them after your teacher.

1 use a credit card

2 worry about money

3 write checks

4 shop at thrift stores

5 buy red socks

6 go to garage sales

7 shop at department stores

8 borrow money

9 buy flowers

10 lose your money

11 return clothes

12 steal things

PAIRWORK. Practice with a partner. Student A, look at this page and say the words. Student B, look at page 59 and point to the pictures.

Listen and Write

3. Listen and complete the sentences.

1. Sometimes I _____ _____ if they're the wrong size.

2. I usually _____ _____ _____ _____ when I go shopping.

3. I like to save money, so I sometimes shop at _____ _____ .

4. My wife and I _____ _____ money all the time!

5. Sometimes I _____ money at the end of the month.

6. Sometimes my husband and I go to _____ _____ .

7. I always _____ _____ _____ because my girlfriend likes red.

8. I don't like to carry money with me, so I _____ _____ a lot.

Conversation

Do you ever _____ ?	Yes, I do.
	No, I don't. / never.

4. Practice the conversations with your teacher.

A: Do you ever write checks?
B: Yes, I do.
A: How often?
B: A lot.

How often?
A lot.
Once in a while.
Not very much.

A: Do you ever use a credit card?
B: No, I don't.

PAIRWORK. Now look at page 59. Make new conversations with a partner.
Ask: 1. *Do you ever...?* 2. *How often?*

Writing Practice

I	often / sometimes / never	_____ .
I don't	_____ .	
	_____ very much.	

5. Write sentences about yourself.

Examples: <u>I often worry about money.</u>

<u>I don't use a credit card very much.</u>

1. _____
2. _____
3. _____
4. _____

Do You Ever Use a Credit Card? **61**

Learn about Your Classmates

Do you like _____?	Do you like to _____?
television	watch television
coffee	drink coffee
music	dance
Chinese food	cook

6. Practice the conversations with your teacher.

A: Do you like to go shopping?
B: Yes, I do.
A: Me too.

A: Do you like American food?
B: No, I don't.
A: Me neither.

A: Do you like to eat at restaurants?
B: Yes, I do.
A: I don't.

PAIRWORK. Now close your book and make new conversations with a partner.

Writing Practice

I like (to) _____.	I don't like (to) _____.

7. Write sentences about yourself.

Examples: I like American movies.

I don't like to wait for the bus.

1. _____

2. _____

3. _____

4. _____

5. _____

6. _____

Calling Stores

8. Susan and Carlos are calling May's Department Store at City Shopping Center. Listen to their conversations. Then practice them with your teacher.

Clerk: May's Department Store. May I help you?
Susan: Yes. Do you sell children's clothes?
Clerk: Yes, we do. They're on the third floor.
Susan: Third floor. Thank you.

Clerk: May's Department Store. May I help you?
Carlos: Yes. Do you sell toys?
Clerk: No, we don't. Try Toy World.
         It's on the fifth floor of the shopping center.
Carlos: Shopping center, fifth floor. Thank you.

9. Does May's Department Store have these things? Listen and check (✔) *Yes* or *No.* Then circle the correct floor of the store or the shopping center.

		Yes	No	Which floor?				
1.		✔	☐	1st	2nd	(3rd)	4th	5th
2.		☐	☐	1st	2nd	3rd	4th	5th
3.		☐	☐	1st	2nd	3rd	4th	5th
4.		☐	☐	1st	2nd	3rd	4th	5th
5.		☐	☐	1st	2nd	3rd	4th	5th
6.		☐	☐	1st	2nd	3rd	4th	5th

Paying the Cashier

10. Learn the new words. Look at the pictures and repeat the words after your teacher.

picture ID

driver's license

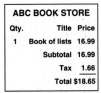

receipt

Listen to the conversation and practice it with your teacher.

Customer: I'd like this iron.
Cashier: OK. How are you paying for this?
Customer: Do you take checks?
Cashier: Yes, with a picture ID.
Customer: I have a driver's license.
Cashier: That's fine. It comes to $27.69.
Customer: Here you are.
Cashier: Thank you. Your receipt is in the bag.

Ways to pay
pay cash
write a check
use a credit card

11. Look at the pictures and write a conversation. Then practice it with a partner.

Customer: _____

Cashier: _____

Customer: _____

Cashier: _____

Customer: _____

Cashier: _____

Customer: _____

Cashier: _____

ABC BOOK STORE		
Qty.	Title	Price
1	Book of lists	16.99
	Subtotal	16.99
	Tax	1.66
	Total	$18.65

Do people write checks in your country? Do people use credit cards?

What Does Ken Do on Weeknights?

1. Look at the pictures. Answer your teacher's questions. (Teacher, see page 203.)

	M T W TH 🌙	FRIDAY 🌙	SATURDAY	SUNDAY

Topic: leisure activities
Life skill: telephone messages
Structure: present tense

Leisure Activities

2. Learn the new words. Listen to the words. Repeat them after your teacher.

① read books

② play cards

③ play soccer

④ go to church

⑤ relax

⑥ go dancing

⑦ run in the park

⑧ not do anything

⑨ do homework

⑩ watch TV

⑪ play with (their) friends

⑫ not do anything

PAIRWORK. Practice with a partner. Student A, look at this page and say the words. Student B, look at page 65 and point to the pictures.

I You We They	read books.	He She	reads books.

Listen and Write

3. Listen and complete the sentences.

1. Every Friday night, Ken _____ _____ .

2. On Saturday afternoons, Judy _____ _____ ____ _____ .

3. Most Saturdays, Linda and Paul _____ _____ _____ _____ .

4. On weeknights, Ken _____ _____ at home.

5. The kids _____ _____ on weeknights.

6. On Saturday, Ken usually _____ _____ in the afternoon.

7. On Sundays, Judy doesn't _____ _____ .

8. The kids usually _____ _____ _____ on Sundays.

Spelling

A. read ⟶ read**s**	C. study ⟶ stud**ies**
	↑ — *consonant*
B. rela**x** ⟶ relax**es**	
wat**ch** ⟶ watch**es**	play ⟶ play**s**
wa**sh** ⟶ wash**es**	↑ — *vowel*
pre**ss** ⟶ press**es**	

have ⟶ **has**	go ⟶ **goes**	do ⟶ **does**

4. Add *-s* to these verbs. Follow the examples above.

1. clean _____   4. have _____   7. miss _____

2. teach _____   5. worry _____   8. fix _____

3. pay _____   6. buy _____   9. go _____

Conversation

What **does**	he she	usually do on _____?	What **do**	you they	usually do on _____?

5. Practice the conversation with your teacher.

A: What does Ken usually do on weeknights?
B: He reads books.
A: What do you do on weeknights?
B: I watch TV.

A: What do the kids usually do on Sunday?
B: They don't do anything.
A: What do you do on Sunday?
B: I work!

PAIRWORK. Now look at page 65. Make new conversations with a partner.

Same meaning	Same meaning
She/He doesn't do anything.	I/They don't do anything.
She/He does nothing.	I/They do nothing.

Writing Practice

She He	plays soccer. goes dancing.	She He	doesn't	play soccer. go dancing.

6. Write sentences about your family or friends.

Examples: ___My husband watches TV in the evenings.___

___My sister doesn't go to church.___

1. _____

2. _____

3. _____

4. _____

5. _____

Now close your book and tell a partner about your family and friends.

He She	likes to doesn't like to	_____ .

7. Write more sentences about your family or friends.

Examples: ___My wife likes to go to the park.___

___My brother doesn't like to speak English.___

1. _____

2. _____

3. _____

4. _____

5. _____

Now close your book and tell your partner about your family and friends.

Phone Messages

8. Listen to the conversation. Then practice it with your teacher.

Mrs. Wong: Hello?
Mr. Sato: Hello. May I please speak to Ken?
Mrs. Wong: I'm sorry, but he's not here now.
He plays soccer on Saturday afternoons.
Would you like to leave a message?
Mr. Sato: Yes, please. Tell him to call Mr. Sato at home.
The number is 982-4463.
Mrs. Wong: 982-4463. OK.
Mr. Sato: Thank you.
Mrs. Wong: You're welcome. Good-bye.

Ken—
Call Mr Sato.
982-4463

9. Listen to the conversations. Complete the messages.

1
Susan —
Call Betsy.
_____

2
Mr. Sato —
Call _____
_____

3
Carlos —
Call _____
_____

4
Linda —
Call _____
_____

5
Carlos —
_____
_____

6
_____
_____
_____

Phone Messages

10. The sentences in this conversation are not in the correct **order.** Number the sentences correctly and write the conversation below. Then practice it with a partner.

___1___ Hello?

_____ The number is 667-3452.

_____ She goes to church on Sunday mornings.

_____ Yes, please. Tell her to call Judy at home.

_____ 667-3452. OK.

___2___ Hello. May I please speak to Eva?

_____ You're welcome. Good-bye.

_____ Would you like to leave a message?

_____ Thank you.

_____ I'm sorry, but she's not here now.

A: _____

B: _____

A: _____

_____

B: _____

_____

A: _____

B: _____

A: _____

11. You are calling a friend. Complete the conversation. Then practice it with your partner.

A: Hello?

B: Hello. May I please speak to_____?

A: I'm sorry, but_____ not here now.

_____.

Would you like to leave a message?

B: Yes, please. Tell_____.

The number is_____ .

A: _____ . OK.

B: Thank you.

A: You're welcome. Good-bye.

Now close your book and make new conversations with your partner.

What do people do in their leisure time in your country?

What Does Judy Do?

1. Look at the pictures. Answer your teacher's questions. (Teacher, see page 204.)

1 Judy	**2** Carlos	**3** Ken	**4** Marsha
5 Tom	**6** Ruth	**7** Lisa	**8** Marco
9 Andy	**10** Joe	**11** Ivan	**12** Peter
13 Tran	**14** Kathy	**15** Tony	**16** Sally

Topic: **occupations**
Life skill: **finding out about jobs**
Structure: **present tense**

71

Jobs and Duties

2. Learn the new words. Listen to the words. Repeat them after your teacher.

1 secretary/receptionist
type letters and answer phones

2 construction worker
build houses and buildings

3 stock clerk
put things on shelves

4 seamstress
sew clothes

5 factory worker
work in a factory

6 mail carrier
deliver mail

7 fire fighter
put out fires

8 police officer
protect people

9 plumber
fix pipes

10 mechanic
repair cars and machines

11 janitor
clean offices and buildings

12 electrician
work with electricity

13 cashier
take money and give change

14 waitress/waiter
serve food

15 security guard
guard stores and banks

16 dentist
take care of our teeth

PAIRWORK. Practice with a partner. Student A, look at this page and say the words. Student B, look at page 71 and point to the pictures.

3. Listen and write the number of each conversation under the correct picture.

Ⓐ

_____ _____

Ⓑ

_____ _____

Ⓒ

_____ _____

Ⓓ

_____ _____

Ⓔ

_____ _____

Ⓕ

_____ _____

Ⓖ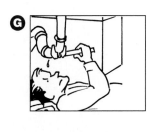

_____ _____

Ⓗ

1   Peter

Ⓘ

_____ _____

Now listen again and write each person's name beside the number.

4. Listen and complete the sentences.

1. My name's Joe, and I repair cars. I'm a _____ .

2. I'm Marsha, and I sew clothes. I'm a _____ .

3. My name is Carlos, and I work on houses. I'm a _____ _____ .

4. I'm Ken. I work as a _____ _____ at the bicycle company.

5. My name is Sally. I take care of people's teeth. I'm a _____ .

6. I'm Andy, and I fix the pipes in people's homes. I'm a _____ .

7. My name is Ivan, and I work cleaning offices. I'm a _____ .

8. I'm Kathy, and I'm a _____ in a restaurant.

5. Practice the conversations with your teacher.

A: What does Marsha do?
B: She's a seamstress.
A: What does she do at work?
B: She sews clothes.

A: What does Joe do?
B: He's a mechanic.
A: What does he do at work?
B: He repairs cars.

PAIRWORK. Now look at page 71. Make new conversations with a partner.

6. Write sentences about yourself and your family or friends.

Example: ___My brother is a mechanic.___
___He fixes cars at work.___

1. ___I am___
   ___I___ _____ at work.

2. ___My___ _____ ___is___
   _____ at work.

3. ___My___
   _____ at work.

4. ___My___
   _____ at work.

5. ___My___
   _____ at work.

7. Do you know what these abbreviations mean? Talk about them with a partner. Then ask your teacher. Write the words on the lines.

1. F/T _____
2. P/T _____
3. perm. _____
4. temp. _____
5. sal. _____

6. $5/hr. _____
7. 6 days/wk. _____
8. appt. _____
9. exp. req. _____
10. no exp. nec. _____

8. You can find out about jobs in Help Wanted ads. Read the ads with your partner and write answers to the questions. Ask your teacher if you don't understand.

HELP WANTED	HELP WANTED	HELP WANTED
CASHIER for Joe's Groceries. P/T, eves. No exp. nec. 1127 Third Ave. No phone calls.	JANITOR Factory needs clean-up person. F/T, 6 pm to 2 am. $6.50/ hr. Call Jim at 555-4682	RECEPTIONIST F/T person w/ good phone skills. Call Sue at 782-9595. Stow Paper Co.
ELECTRICIAN Temp. F/T job w/ construction co. 4 yrs. exp. req. Call 464-2335 for appt.	MECHANIC Perm. F/T job. Exp. req. $14/hr. A-1 Auto Works, 809 Polk St. No calls.	WAITRESS Ray's Bar and Grill. Perm. P/T, 3 days/wk. Call Ray for appt. 555-8006.

1. Who can you call about the receptionist job? _Sue_____

   What is the name of the company? _Stow Paper Company_____

2. Is the electrician job permanent? _____

   How much experience is required? _____

3. Is the mechanic job full time or part time? _____

   What is the salary? _____

4. What do you do if you want the cashier job? _____

   How much experience is required? _____

5. Where is the waitress job? _____

   How many days a week is the job? _____

6. What are **the hours** of the janitor job? _____

   What do you do if you want the janitor job? _____

Job Qualifications

9. Read the Help Wanted ads with your teacher. Then listen to people talk about their job qualifications. Circle *yes* if the person can do the job. Circle *no* if the person can't do the job.

Can he or she do the job?

	HELP WANTED		
1. Andy	PLUMBER Office bldgs, homes. 5 yrs. exp. Must have driver's license and tools. 555-2839	(yes)	no
2. Kathy	SEAMSTRESS Clothing factory needs person for nite shift. Exp. req. Call Mrs. Baker at 367-4280.	yes	no
3. Debbie	SECRETARY for import co. Must speak English and Chinese. Exp. w/ computers req. Call 839-7116.	yes	no
4. Tony	CONSTRUCTION WORK, F/T Exp. req. Must have truck and tools. Call Mr. Snow at 555-9732.	yes	no
5. Ken	STOCK CLERK for Riverside Supermarket. Must lift heavy things. No exp. nec. 4010 River Street. No calls.	yes	no

10. Can you do any of the jobs on pages 75 and 76? Complete the sentences below with information about yourself.

1. (Occupation) I am a _____.

2. (F/T or P/T) I want a _____ job.

3. (Skills) I can _____.

4. (Experience) I have _____ years' experience.

5. (Hours) I can work _____.

PAIRWORK. Now tell your qualifications to a partner.

How do people find jobs in your country?

Can You Drive a Truck?

1. Look at the pictures. Answer your teacher's questions. (Teacher, see page 204.)

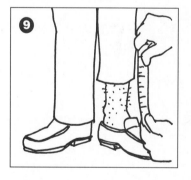

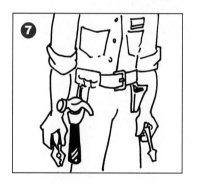

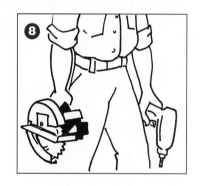

Topic: work skills
Life skill: calling for a job interview
Structure: modal *can*

Job Skills

2. Learn the new words. Listen to the words. Repeat them after your teacher.

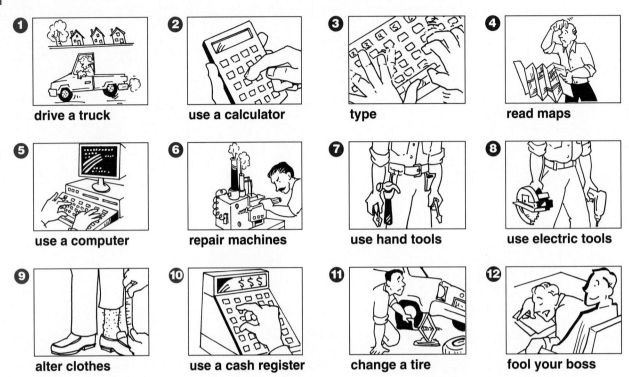

① drive a truck

② use a calculator

③ type

④ read maps

⑤ use a computer

⑥ repair machines

⑦ use hand tools

⑧ use electric tools

⑨ alter clothes

⑩ use a cash register

⑪ change a tire

⑫ fool your boss

PAIRWORK. Practice with a partner. Student A, look at this page and say the words. Student B, look at page 77 and point to the pictures.

Listen and Write

3. Listen and complete the sentences.

1. All the people in my office can _____ .

2. My sister likes to sew, and she can _____ _____ .

3. I use machines, but I can't _____ _____ .

4. Be careful when you use _____ _____ !

5. When you travel, it's important to _____ _____ .

6. I like to make things, so I often use _____ _____ .

7. These days, most people can use _____ _____ .

8. I can only drive a car, but my sister can _____ _____ _____ .

Conversation

| Can you _____ ? | Yes, I can.
No, I can't. |

4. Practice the conversation with your teacher.

A: Can you type?
B: Yes, I can.
A: Do you type at work?
B: Yes, I do.

A: Can you drive a truck?
B: Yes, I can.
A: Do you drive a truck at work?
B: No, I don't.

A: Can you repair machines?
B: No, I can't.

PAIRWORK. Now look at page 77. Make new conversations with a partner.

Writing Practice

5. Write about your skills. Ask your teacher if you need help.

Example: I can cook for many people.

1. _____

2. _____

3. _____

Now write about things you can't do but want to learn.

Example: I can't fix cars, but I want to learn.

1. _____

2. _____

3. _____

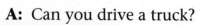

Do You Know How to Type?

Do you know how to _____?	Yes, I do. No, I don't.

6. Practice the conversation with your teacher.

A: Do you know how to type?
B: Yes, I do. I have four years' experience.

A: Do you know how to use a computer?
B: No, I don't, but I learn quickly.

PAIRWORK. Now look at page 77. Make new conversations with a partner.

Writing Practice

7. Write about your skills. Ask your teacher if you need help.

Example: _I know how to type. I have four years' experience._

1. _____

2. _____

3. _____

Now write about things you don't know how to do.

Example: _I don't know how to use a computer, but I learn quickly._

1. _____

2. _____

3. _____

Calling for a Job Interview

8. Read the Help Wanted ad from the newspaper.

> CONSTRUCTION WORK
> A-1 Builders. Exp. req.
> Call Mr. Mills, 555-0806

Carlos is calling about the job with A-1 Builders. Listen to his conversation. Then practice it with your teacher.

Receptionist: A-1 Builders.
Carlos: Hello. May I please speak to Mr. Mills?
Receptionist: Just a minute, please.
Mr. Mills: This is Mr. Mills.
Carlos: Hello. My name is Carlos Gomez. I'm calling about the job as a construction worker. I have ten years' experience.
Mr. Mills: I see. Can you come in for an interview?
Carlos: Yes, I can. When?
Mr. Mills: How about tomorrow afternoon at three o'clock?
Carlos: Tomorrow at three is fine. What's the address?
Mr. Mills: 808 Leigh Avenue.
Carlos: 808 Leigh? Can you spell that, please?
Mr. Mills: Sure. It's L-e-i-g-h.
Carlos: L-e-i-g-h. OK, Mr. Mills. I'll be there at three tomorrow.

9. Read these Help Wanted ads.

| CASHIER for May's Cafeteria. Exp. req. Call May at 864-0369. | MECHANIC Exp.req. Joe's Auto Works. Call Joe at 555-5655. | SECRETARY Pacific Travel. Must speak Chinese. Mrs. Lo, 246-1190. | SECURITY GUARD Eastside Bank. Nite shift. Call Mr. Tong, 466-2189. |

Listen to people calling for job interviews. Circle the correct job. Then write the day and time of the interview and the address.

Job		Day and Time	Address
1. cashier secretary	(mechanic) security guard	_____	
2. cashier secretary	mechanic security guard	_____	
3. cashier secretary	mechanic security guard	_____	
4. cashier secretary	mechanic security guard	_____	

10. Choose one of the job ads on page 81 and write a conversation with a partner. Use the addresses below.

> May's Cafeteria, 2205 Jayne Street
> Joe's Auto Works, 1227 Brewer Street
> Pacific Travel, 764 Gough Street
> Eastside Bank, 92 Boren Avenue

Receptionist: _____ .

You: Hello. May I please _____ ?

Receptionist: Just _____ .

Employer: This is _____ .

You: Hello. _____ .

I'm calling about _____ .

I _____ .

Employer: I see. _____ ?

You: Yes, I can. When?

Employer: How about _____ ?

You: _____ .

What's the address?

Employer: _____ .

You: _____ ? Can you _____ ?

Employer: Sure. It's _____ .

You: _____ . OK, _____ .

I'll be there _____ .

Practice the conversation with your partner. Take turns being the person calling about the job.

 Do you use the telephone to find out about jobs in your country?

UNIT 14

Where Does Carlos Work?

1. Look at the pictures. Answer your teacher's questions. (Teacher, see page 204.)

Work Time

at Talbot
Construction

by bus

at 8:30

5 days

8 hours

every two
weeks

on Friday

Free Time

relax

his family

on the
weekend

downtown

love stories

an hour a day

once a week

funny movies

Topic: **habitual activities**
Life skill: **job interviews**
Structure: **modal *have to***

83

Asking about Habits

2. Read the questions and answers. Repeat them after your teacher.

 1. **Where** does Carlos work? at Talbot Construction

 2. **A. How** does he get to work? **A.** by bus
    B. What time does he get to work? **B.** at 8:30

 3. **A. How many** days does he work? **A.** 5 days
    B. How many hours does he work? **B.** 8 hours

 4. **A. How often** does he get paid? **A.** every two weeks
    B. What day does he get paid? **B.** on Friday

 5. **A. What** does he do after work? **A.** relax
    B. Who does he relax **with**? **B.** his family

 6. **A. When** does he go shopping? **A.** on the weekend
    B. Where does he go shopping? **B.** downtown

 7. **A. What kind** of things does he read? **A.** love stories
    B. How much time does he read every day? **B.** an hour a day
    (**How long** does he read every day?)

 8. **A. How often** does he go to the movies? **A.** once a week
    B. What kind of movies does he see? **B.** funny movies

Conversation

3. Listen to Susan talk with her new neighbor. Then practice the conversation with your teacher.

8:30

A: What time **does** Carlos get to work?
B: At eight thirty.
A: What time **do** you get to work?
B: At eight o'clock. What about you?
A: Around seven thirty.

love stories

A: What kind of things does Carlos read?
B: Love stories.
A: What kind of things do you read?
B: **Magazines.** How about you?
A: Funny books.

on the weekend

A: When does Carlos go shopping?
B: On the weekend.
A: When do you go shopping?
B: The same. On the weekend. What about you?
A: I never go shopping. My husband does the shopping.
B: Lucky you!

PAIRWORK. Now look at page 83. Make new conversations with a partner.

4. After you finish talking, write sentences about your partner.

Examples: <u>Juan gets paid every week.</u>

<u>He usually goes shopping after work.</u>

1. _____

2. _____

3. _____

4. _____

5. _____

5. Read about how to find a job. Ask your teacher if you don't understand.

If you want a job in the United States, here are some things you **have to** do. First, you have to find out about jobs. You can look in the newspaper in the Help Wanted ads, or you can ask about jobs at the employment office. You can also ask your friends. Second, when you find a job you want, you have to **apply** for it. Sometimes you go to the company **in person**. Other times, you have to call and make an **appointment**. At most places, you have to **fill out** an **application form**. At some places, you also have to have an interview. In the interview, the **employer** asks about your work experience, skills, and education, and you have to answer the questions.

If the employer likes you, he or she **may hire** you right away. If the employer doesn't hire you right away, he or she may call you when there is a job available.

Now write answers to the questions.

1. What three ways can you find out about jobs?

   a. _Look in the Help Wanted ads._____

   b. _____

   c. _____

2. What do you have to do when you find a job you want?

   _____

3. When you call the employer, what do you ask for?

   _____

4. At the company, what two things do you often have to do?

   a. _____

   b. _____

5. In the interview, what do you have to talk about?

   _____

6. What does the employer do if he or she likes you?

   _____

6. Close your book and tell a partner how to find a job in your country. Start like this: "If you want a job in my country, you have to…"

Talk and Write

7. Talk with your classmates and teacher about what people have to do and don't have to do.

1. Children have to do these things.

go to school

_____

_____

_____

_____

2. Children don't have to do these things.

go to work

_____

_____

_____

_____

3. Adults have to do these things.

_____

_____

_____

_____

4. Adults don't have to do these things.

_____

_____

_____

_____

Now write sentences about yourself.

Examples: _I have to speak English at my job._

I don't have to get up early on Sundays.

1. _____

2. _____

3. _____

4. _____

5. _____

6. _____

Job Interviews

8. Carlos is looking for a new job. Listen to his job interview with Mr. Mills. Then practice it with your teacher and with a partner.

Mr. Mills:	Carlos, are you looking for a part-time job or a full-time job?
Carlos:	A full-time job.
Mr. Mills:	Do you have experience as a construction worker?
Carlos:	Yes, I do. I have ten years' experience.
Mr. Mills:	Where do you work now?
Carlos:	At Talbot Construction.
Mr. Mills:	Can you lift heavy things?
Carlos:	Yes, I can. I'm **strong** and **healthy**.
Mr. Mills:	When can you start work for us?
Carlos:	Next week.

9. For each question, read the answers first with your teacher. Then listen to the question and circle the letter of the correct answer.

1. a. Yes, I am.
 b. On Monday.
 c. Yes, I can. *(circled)*

2. a. At ABC Bookstore.
 b. From 8:00 A.M. to 5:00 P.M.
 c. Yes, I do.

3. a. Two years' experience.
 b. Yes, I am.
 c. At a bicycle factory.

4. a. Next Monday.
 b. No, I can't.
 c. At May's Department Store.

5. a. Yes, I am.
 b. Yes, I do.
 c. On the weekend.

6. a. Yes, I do.
 b. Five years' experience.
 c. Next week.

7. a. No, I'm not.
 b. At night.
 c. No, I can't.

8. a. Yes, I do.
 b. A full-time job.
 c. Right away.

9. a. Yes, I can.
 b. No, I'm not.
 c. Next month.

10. a. At a sewing factory.
 b. Three years' experience.
 c. Yes, I do.

Medical Advice

7. Learn the new words. Look at the pictures and repeat the words after your teacher.

cavity

infection

shot

thermometer

Mrs. Sato isn't feeling well. Listen to her conversation with Judy. Then practice it with your teacher.

Judy:	Hi, Mrs. Sato. How are you?
Mrs. Sato:	Hi, Judy. I'm not feeling very well.
Judy:	What's the matter?
Mrs. Sato:	I have a sore throat.
Judy:	Why don't you see a doctor? **Maybe** you have an infection.
Mrs. Sato:	An infection? Hmm. Maybe you're right. Thanks for the advice.

8. Judy's coworkers aren't feeling well. Listen to the conversations and put a check (✔) above the correct health problem.

	Problem	Advice
1. Susan	✔	See a dentist. Maybe you have a ___cavity___.
2. Ivan		See a doctor. Maybe you need a _____.
3. Mr. Sato		Take your temperature with this _____. Maybe you have a fever.
4. Ruth		See a doctor. Maybe you have an _____.
5. Ken		Go home. Maybe you need some _____.

Now listen again. Complete Judy's advice.

What's the Matter with Susan? **95**

Medical Advice

9. Listen to the conversation and write the missing words. Then practice the conversation with a partner.

Judy: Hi, Carlos. How are you?

Carlos: Hi, Judy. I'm not feeling very well.

Judy: What's the _____?

Carlos: I feel hot and _____ .

Judy: Why don't you take your _____ with this thermometer?

Maybe you have a _____ .

Carlos: A _____? Hmm. Maybe you're right.

Thanks for the _____ .

10. Write a new conversation with your partner. One student has a health problem. The other student gives advice.

A: Hi, _____ . How are you?

B: Hi, _____ . _____ .

A: _____ ?

B: _____ .

A: _____ ?

_____ .

B: _____? Hmm. _____ .

_____ .

Practice the conversation with your partner. Then make new conversations about other health problems.

At the Drugstore

INFORMATION GAP. Work with a partner. Student A, look at this page. Student B, look at page 98.

11. Learn the new words. Look at the pictures and repeat the words after your teacher.

pill (tablet)   capsule   teaspoon   tablespoon

Read the **labels** with your teacher. Then practice the conversations with your teacher and a partner.

Antacid
(for stomach problems)
Dosage: 2 capsules
twice a day

Customer: How much antacid do I take?
Druggist: Two capsules.
Customer: How often?
Druggist: Twice a day.

Cough Medicine

Dosage: 1 tablespoon
every 4 hours

Customer: How much cough medicine do I take?
Druggist: One tablespoon.
Customer: How often?
Druggist: Every four hours.

12. Student A, you are the customer. Student B is the druggist. Ask the druggist about the medicines on the top and write the information on the labels. Then change: Student A, you are the druggist, and Student B is the customer. Answer the customer's questions about the medicines on the bottom.

Aspirin

Dosage: _____

_____

Diarrhea Medicine

Dosage: _____

_____

Cough Medicine

Dosage: _____

_____

Antacid

Dosage: 2 tablespoons
every 4 hours

Cold Medicine

Dosage: 1 tablet
twice a day

Diarrhea Medicine

Dosage: 1 capsule
3 times a day

 Is medicine in the United States different from medicine in your country?

At the Drugstore

INFORMATION GAP. Work with a partner. Student B, look at this page. Student A, look at page 97.

11. Learn the new words. Look at the pictures and repeat the words after your teacher.

pill (tablet)   capsule   teaspoon   tablespoon

Read the **labels** with your teacher. Then practice the conversations with your teacher and a partner.

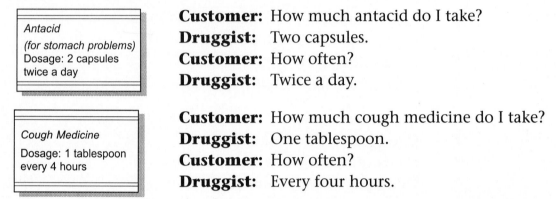

Antacid *(for stomach problems)* Dosage: 2 capsules twice a day	**Customer:** How much antacid do I take? **Druggist:** Two capsules. **Customer:** How often? **Druggist:** Twice a day.
Cough Medicine Dosage: 1 tablespoon every 4 hours	**Customer:** How much cough medicine do I take? **Druggist:** One tablespoon. **Customer:** How often? **Druggist:** Every four hours.

12. Student B, you are the druggist. Student A is the customer. Answer the customer's questions about the medicines on the top. Then change: Student B, you are the customer, and Student A is the druggist. Ask the druggist about the medicines on the bottom and write the information on the labels.

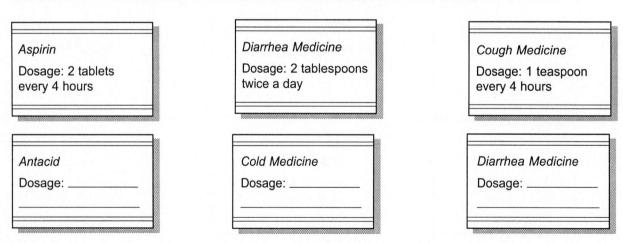

Aspirin

Dosage: 2 tablets
every 4 hours

Diarrhea Medicine

Dosage: 2 tablespoons
twice a day

Cough Medicine

Dosage: 1 teaspoon
every 4 hours

Antacid

Dosage: _____

_____

Cold Medicine

Dosage: _____

_____

Diarrhea Medicine

Dosage: _____

_____

Is medicine in the United States different from medicine in your country?

Is Carlos Going to Go to Work on Thursday?

1. Look at the pictures. Answer your teacher's questions. (Teacher, see page 205.)

	TUESDAY	WEDNESDAY	THURSDAY

Topic: **health problems**
Life skill: **calling in sick**
Structure: future *going to*

99

Ups and Downs

2. Learn the new words. Listen to the words. Repeat them after your teacher.

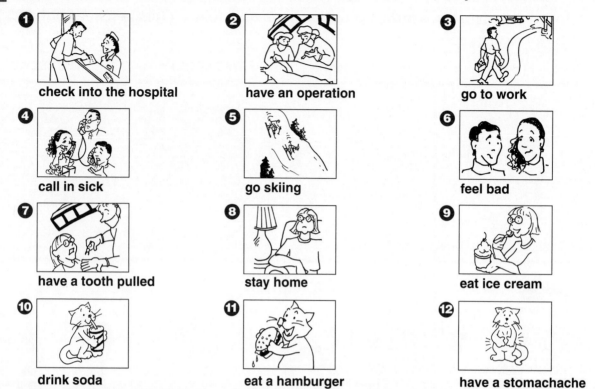

1 check into the hospital

2 have an operation

3 go to work

4 call in sick

5 go skiing

6 feel bad

7 have a tooth pulled

8 stay home

9 eat ice cream

10 drink soda

11 eat a hamburger

12 have a stomachache

PAIRWORK. Practice with a partner. Student A, look at this page and say the words. Student B, look at page 99 and point to the pictures.

Listen and Write

3. Listen and complete the sentences.

1. Next Wednesday, Ken and Judy are going to _____ _____ .

2. Susan is going to _____ _____ next Wednesday.

3. Carlos is going to _____ _____ _____ next Wednesday.

4. Next Tuesday, the cat is going to _____ _____ .

5. Carlos is going to _____ _____ _____ _____ next Tuesday.

6. Susan is going to_____ _____ _____ _____ next Tuesday.

7. Are Ken and Judy going to _____ _____ on Thursday?

8. Is Susan going to _____ _____ _____ on Thursday?

Conversation

What's	he she	going to do_____?	He's She's They're	going to_____.
What **are** they				

Is	he she	going to _____?	Yes, he/she is. No, he/she isn't.
Are they			Yes, they are. No, they aren't.

4. Practice the conversations with your teacher.

1.

A: What's Carlos going to do next Tuesday?
B: He's going to check into the hospital.

2.

A: What's he going to do on Wednesday?
B: He's going to have an operation.

3.

A: Is he going to go to work on Thursday?
B: Yes, he is. *or* No, he isn't.

4.

A: What are Ken and Judy going to do next Tuesday?
B: They're going to call in sick.

5.

A: What are they going to do on Wednesday?
B: They're going to go skiing.

6.

A: Are they going to feel bad on Thursday?
B: Yes, they are. *or* No, they aren't.

PAIRWORK. Now look at page 99. Make new conversations with a partner.

She's He's They're	going to _____ .	She isn't He isn't They aren't	going to _____ .

5. Write sentences about next week. Give your own **opinion** about Thursday.

Examples: On Tuesday, Carlos is going to check into the hospital.

On Wednesday, he's going to have an operation.

1. On Thursday, _____
2. On Tuesday, Ken and Judy _____
3. _____
4. _____
5. On Tuesday, Susan _____
6. _____
7. _____
8. On Tuesday, the cat _____
9. _____
10. _____

Learn about Your Classmates

What are you going to do _____ ?	I'm going to _____ .

6. Practice the conversations with your teacher.

A: What are you going to do after school today?
B: I'm going to go home. How about you?
A: I'm going to go to work.

A: What are you going to do next weekend?
B: I'm going to see a movie. What about you?
A: I'm going to go to the park.

PAIRWORK. Close your book. Ask a partner about *after school today,* *next weekend,* **and** *next summer.*

Writing Practice

> I'm going to _____.
>
> I'm not going to _____.

7. Write sentences about next weekend. Tell three things you're going to do and three things you aren't going to do.

Examples: <u>I'm going to visit my uncle.</u>

<u>I'm not going to go dancing.</u>

1. <u>I'm going to _____</u>

2. _____

3. _____

4. <u>I'm not going to _____</u>

5. _____

6. _____

Calling in Sick

 8. Susan is calling in sick. Listen to the conversation and practice it with your teacher.

Judy: Ace Bicycle Factory. Judy speaking.

Susan: Hello, Judy. This is Susan Gomez.
I'm not going to come to work today. I'm sick.

Judy: Oh, no. What's the matter?

Susan: I have a fever and chills. **I think** I have the flu.

Judy: I'm sorry to hear that.
Are you going to come in tomorrow?

Susan: I'm not sure.

Judy: OK. I hope you feel better soon.

Susan: Thanks. Good-bye.

9. Do you remember these health problems? Repeat the words after your teacher.

| ear infection |
| cramps |
| cavity |
| chills |
| throat infection |

Listen to other Ace Bicycle Factory **employees** call in sick to work. Write their health problems. Then circle *yes*, *no*, or *not sure*.

	Problem	Going to come in tomorrow?		
1. Ivan	*throat infection*	yes	(no)	not sure
2. Ruth	_____	yes	no	not sure
3. Mr. Sato	_____	yes	no	not sure
4. Tran	_____	yes	no	not sure
5. Marco	_____	yes	no	not sure

10. You are calling in sick to work. Complete the conversation. Then practice it with a partner.

A: _____ . _____ speaking.

B: Hello, _____ . This is _____ .

I'm not _____ . I'm sick.

A: Oh, no. What's _____ ?

B: _____ .

A: I'm sorry to hear that.

Are you _____ ?

B: _____ .

A: OK. I hope _____ .

B: _____ . Good-bye.

In your country, what are some reasons that people take time off from work?

When Is Ken Going to Move?

1. Look at the pictures. Answer your teacher's questions. (Teacher, see page 206.)

	FRIDAY	SATURDAY

  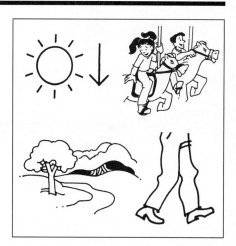

Topic: housing
Life skill: ordering services
Structure: future *going to*

2. Learn the new words. Listen to the sentences. Repeat them after your teacher.

 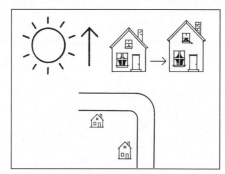 

1. On Friday morning, Ken's going to move to a new apartment around the corner.

2. On Saturday, he's going to buy four chairs with Judy.
He's going to take them home in his car.

3. On Friday night, the kids are going to see a movie downtown with their parents.

4. On Saturday afternoon, they're going to ride a merry-go-round at the park.
They're going to walk there.

5. On Friday, the cat's going to play checkers all day with the parrot in the living room.

6. On Saturday, he's not going to do anything. (He's going to do nothing.)

PAIRWORK. Now look at page 105. Make sentences with a partner.

| Wh _____ | is he
is she
are they | going to _____ ? |

3. Practice the conversations with your teacher.

1.  **A: What** is Ken going to do on Saturday?
B: He's going to buy chairs for his new apartment.

2.  **A: How many** chairs is he going to buy?
B: Four.

3.  **A: Who** is he going to buy the chairs **with**?
B: Judy.

4.  **A: How** is he going to take the chairs home?
B: In his car.

5.  **A: What** are the kids going to do on Saturday?
B: They're going to ride on a merry-go-round.

6.  **A: Where** are they going to ride the merry-go-round?
B: At the park.

7. 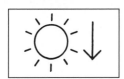 **A: When** are they going to go to the park?
B: In the afternoon.

8.  **A: How** are they going to get to the park?
B: They're going to walk there.

PAIRWORK. Now look at page 105. Make new conversations with a partner.

Wh _____ are you going to _____ ?

4. **Practice the conversation with your teacher.**

A: What are you going to do next weekend?
B: I'm going to have a barbecue.

A: Where are you going to have the barbecue?
B: In the park.

A: What day are you going to have it?
B: On Sunday.

A: What time are you going to go to the park?
B: Around five o'clock.

A: Who are you going to have the barbecue with?
B: My family and my sister's family.

A: How are you going to get to the park?
B: We're going to drive there.

PAIRWORK. Now close your book and ask a partner about next weekend or next summer.

Ask: 1. *What?* 2. *Where?* 3. *What day?* 4. *What time?* 5. *Who. . .with?* 6. *How?*

After you finish talking, write about your partner's plans.

Example: ___Mei is going to see a movie on Sunday._____

1. _____

2. _____

3. _____

4. _____

5. _____

Ordering Services

5. Do you remember these services? Repeat the words after your teacher.

gas	electricity
telephone	garbage

Listen to Ken's conversation with the gas company. Then practice it with your teacher.

Receptionist: City Gas Company. May I help you?
Ken: Yes. I'd like service for my new apartment.
Receptionist: Do you have an **account** with us now?
Ken: No, I don't.
Receptionist: What's your name?
Ken: Ken Wong.
Receptionist: What's the address?
Ken: 3506 Baker Street, Apartment 104.
Receptionist: When are you going to move?
Ken: November 1st.
Receptionist: All right, Mr. Wong. There's a **deposit** of $40.
Ken: $40. Thank you. Good-bye.

6. Listen to other people ordering services. Check (✔) the correct service and write the date of the move.

	Service		Date of move	Deposit?	Amount
1.	☐ gas ☐ electricity ✔ garbage ☐ telephone		March 15	(yes) no	$ 25
2.	☐ gas ☐ electricity ☐ garbage ☐ telephone		_____	yes no	$ ____
3.	☐ gas ☐ electricity ☐ garbage ☐ telephone		_____	yes no	$ ____
4.	☐ gas ☐ electricity ☐ garbage ☐ telephone		_____	yes no	$ ____
5.	☐ gas ☐ electricity ☐ garbage ☐ telephone		_____	yes no	$ ____

Listen again. Is there a deposit? Circle *yes* or *no*. If you circle *yes*, write the amount.

7. Look at this utility bill with a partner. Ask your teacher if you don't understand. Then write answers to the questions below.

Western Gas & Electricity

Please write amount of payment

Account Number	Balance Due	Payment Due Date
KHU58 94732-2	35.33	10/14/96

$ _____

Make check payable to:

Western Gas & Electricity
58 Market Street
Los Angeles, CA   90294

Carlos Gomez
1029 22nd Street
Los Angeles, CA   90118

Please enclose top portion with payment.

- -

Western Gas & Electricity

Type of Service	Service Period	Billing Days	Amount
Gas	8/15 – 9/15	31	$16.81
Electricity	8/15 – 9/15	31	$17.50
		Tax	$ 1.02

Questions? Call our office!
(310) 468–9590
58 Market Street
Los Angeles, CA   90294

Current Charges Due	$35.33
Previous balance	$32.44
9/11 Payment	–$32.44
TOTAL AMOUNT DUE	$35.33

Thank you!

---

1. Who is this bill addressed to? _____

2. What utilities is he paying for? _____

3. What is the name of the utility company? _____

4. What is the account number? _____

5. How much does Carlos **owe** for service this month? _____

6. When is the payment due? _____

7. If Carlos doesn't understand the bill, what can he do? _____

8. What is Carlos going to send in the envelope? _____

 Do people move more often in your country or in the United States?

UNIT 18 Will I Be Rich?

1. Look at the pictures. Answer your teacher's questions. (Teacher, see page 206.)

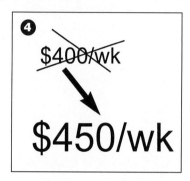

$400/wk

$450/wk

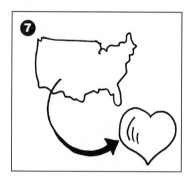

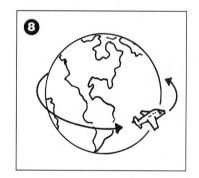

Topic: **predictions**
Life skill: **asking a favor**
Structure: **future will**

In the Future

2. Learn the new words. Listen to the words. Repeat them after your teacher.

1. be rich
2. be famous
3. meet the president
4. get a raise
5. get a promotion
6. get a new job
7. go back to my country
8. travel around the world
9. go to the moon
10. have great-grandchildren
11. have white hair

PAIRWORK. Practice with a partner. Student A, look at this page and say the words. Student B, look at page 111 and point to the pictures.

Listen and Write

3. Listen and complete the sentences.

1. Sometimes I feel lonely here. Will I go back to _____ _____ someday?

2. When I get old, will I have _____ _____ ?

3. My pay is so low! When will I _____ ____ _____ ?

4. I want to see many places. Will I _____ _____ the world someday?

5. I always work hard. When will I get _____ _____ ?

6. I don't like to be poor! Will I _____ _____ in the future?

7. My work isn't very interesting. When will I get a _____ _____ ?

8. I always see the president on TV. _____ ____ _____ him in my lifetime?

Conversation

| Will I _____ ? | Yes, you will.
Probably. (I think so.)
Probably not. (I don't think so.)
No, you won't. | won't = will not |
| When will I _____ ? | | |

4. Ken is talking to a fortune-teller. Listen to the conversation. Then practice it with your teacher.

Ken: Will I travel around the world someday?
Fortune-teller: Yes, you will.
Ken: When will I travel around the world?
Fortune-teller: When you're fifty years old.

Ken: Will I get a raise soon?
Fortune-teller: Probably.
Ken: Wow! When will I get a raise?
Fortune-teller: Next year.

$400/wk
$450/wk

Ken: Will I be famous in the future?
Fortune-teller: I don't think so.

PAIRWORK. Look at page 111. Make new conversations with a partner. Take turns asking questions and being the fortune-teller. Ask: 1. *Will I ...?* and 2. *When?*

Writing Practice

5. Write more questions that you want to know the answer to.

Examples: Will I have a big family?

When will I see my sister again?

1. _____

2. _____

3. _____

4. _____

Possibilities

6. **Read the sentences with your teacher.**

If it's sunny this weekend, I**'ll** go to the park.
If I'm very busy tomorrow, I probably **won't** come to class.

'll = will

Talk with your teacher and classmates about different ways to finish the sentences below. Then write your own answers.

1. If I get a big raise at work, _____

2. If I get a headache tonight, _____

3. If I have a vacation next summer, _____

4. If my kitchen faucet gets a leak, _____

5. If I get a free airplane ticket, _____

6. If it's nice out next Sunday, _____

7. If it's rainy next Sunday, _____

8. If I lose my housekeys tonight, _____

9. If I don't understand something in class today, _____

Learn about Your Classmates

7. **PAIRWORK. Finish the questions below and ask a partner your questions. Then write your partner's answer to each question.**

Example: Question: What will you do if _you find $1,000 on the street?_

Your partner's answer: _I'll buy a diamond ring for my wife._

1. Question: What will you do if _____

   Your partner's answer: _____

2. Question: What will you do if _____

   Your partner's answer: _____

3. Question: What will you do if _____

   Your partner's answer: _____

4. Question: What will you do if _____

   Your partner's answer: _____

Borrowing

8. Susan and her friend Sally are talking. Listen to their conversation. Then practice it with your teacher.

Sally: Hi, Susan.
Susan: Hi, Sally. How are you?
Sally: I'm fine, thanks. Susan, can you **do me a favor?**
Susan: What is it?
Sally: Can I **borrow** your iron? I have to press my clothes.
Susan: My iron? Sure. I'll get it for you right now. ...Here you go.
Sally: Thanks. I'll return it this afternoon. See you later.
Susan: Good-bye.

9. Listen to Susan's conversations with friends and family. Put a check (✔) above the thing each person wants to borrow. Then write when the person will return it.

1.   _tomorrow_ _____

2.   _____

3.   _____

4.   _____

5.   _____

6.   _____

7.   _____

8.   _____

Borrowing

10. Read the conversation with your teacher. Then practice it with a partner.

Sally: Hi, Susan.
Susan: Hi, Sally. How are you?
Sally: I'm fine, thanks. Susan, can you do me a favor?
Susan: What is it?
Sally: Can I borrow your typewriter? I have to type a paper.
Susan: My typewriter? I'm sorry, but I **need** it for work this afternoon.
Sally: That's OK. I'll find another one. See you later.
Susan: Good-bye.

11. Work with your partner and complete the conversations about borrowing things. Then practice the conversations with your partner.

1. **A:** Hi, _____.

   B: Hi, _____. How are you?

   A: _____, _____. _____?

   B: What is it?

   A: Can I _____? I have to _____.

   B: My _____? Sure. _____.
   Here _____.

   A: Thanks. _____. See you later.

   B: _____.

2. **A:** Hi, _____.

   B: Hi, _____. How are you?

   A: _____, _____. _____?

   B: What is it?

   A: Can I _____? I have to _____.

   B: My _____? I'm sorry, but _____.

   A: That's OK. _____. _____.

   B: Good-bye.

 In your country, what things do people borrow from their neighbors?

What Did Carlos Do on Monday?

1. Look at the pictures. Answer your teacher's questions. (Teacher, see page 207.)

Topic: banking
Life skill: opening an account
Structure: past tense

117

Last Week

2. Learn the new words. Listen to the words. Repeat them after your teacher.

① open a bank account

② deposit money

③ shop all day

④ close the bank account

⑤ borrow money

⑥ travel to Las Vegas

⑦ gamble all day

⑧ return the money

⑨ look at mice

⑩ chase mice

⑪ cook the mice

⑫ do nothing

PAIRWORK. Practice with a partner. Student A, look at this page and say the words. Student B, look at page 117 and point to the pictures.

Listen and Write

3. Listen and complete the questions.

1. When did Ken and Judy _____ _____?

2. What day did Carlos _____ _____ _____account?

3. Why did the cat _____ _____ on Tuesday?

4. Where did Ken and Judy_____ _____ _____ ?

5. Why did Carlos close the _____ _____?

6. What day did Ken and Judy _____ _____ _____?

7. Where did Carlos _____ _____ _____ ?

8. When did Carlos _____ _____ in his account?

Talking about the Past

| Every night I wait for the bus.
 Every day I watch TV. | Last night I wait**ed** for the bus.
 Yesterday I watch**ed** TV. |

4. Listen to the examples below. Repeat them after your teacher.

Short sound	Long sound
looked	visi**ted**
shopped	deposi**ted**
traveled	guar**ded**
played	ad**ded**

Practice pronouncing the words with your classmates and teacher.
Circle *S* (short sound) or *L* (long sound) for each word.

1. added	S ⓛ	5. corrected	S L	9. needed	S L	13. started	S L
2. answered	S L	6. ended	S L	10. rented	S L	14. waited	S L
3. borrowed	S L	7. lived	S L	11. repeated	S L	15. wanted	S L
4. closed	S L	8. looked	S L	12. returned	S L	16. washed	S L

Conversation

| What **did** | he <br> she <br> they | do on _____? |

5. Practice the conversation with your teacher.

A: What did Carlos do on Monday?
B: He opened a bank account.

A: What did Ken and Judy do on Thursday?
B: They returned the money.

A: What did the cat do on Thursday?
B: He didn't do anything.

Same meaning
He/She/They didn't do anything.   He/She/They did nothing.

PAIRWORK. Now look at page 117. Make new conversations with a partner.

A. look ⟶ look**ed**	C. *One syllable:*
close ⟶ clos**ed**	shop ⟶ sho**pp**ed
B. stud**y** ⟶ stud**ied**	↑↑ ⎿ *1 consonant*
⎿ *consonant*	⎿ *1 vowel*
play ⟶ play**ed**	*More than one syllable:*
⎿ *vowel*	open ⟶ open**ed**

6. Add *-ed* to these verbs. Follow the examples above.

1. return _____
2. deposit _____
3. stop _____
4. cook _____
5. dry _____

6. argue _____
7. travel _____
8. worry _____
9. stay _____
10. borrow _____

11. visit _____
12. play _____
13. cry _____
14. drop _____
15. move _____

Writing Practice

7. Write about things you and your family or friends did **recently.**
Use verbs from the box.

argue	exercise	stay home	wash
clean	fix	study	watch
cook	kiss	visit	work

Examples: _I cooked chicken for dinner on Saturday._

My children watched television last night.

1. _____
2. _____
3. _____
4. _____
5. _____

At the Post Office

9. Carlos is at the post office. Listen to his conversation with the mail clerk. Then practice it with your teacher.

Clerk: Next, please.
Carlos: Hello. This notice was on my front door yesterday.
Clerk: Let's see. Yes. We have a parcel for you.
I'll go get it. And I'll need to see a picture ID.
(He goes to get the parcel.)
I'm sorry, sir. The parcel isn't here yet.
Carlos: When can I **pick it up?**
Clerk: Come back tomorrow after 10:00 A.M.
Carlos: Thank you.

10. Listen to other conversations at the post office. Check (✔) the correct kind of mail. If the customers pick up their mail, circle *yes*. If they don't pick it up, circle *no* and write when they can come back.

Kind of mail	Pick it up?		Come back when?
1. ✔ magazine			
❏ letter			
❏ parcel	yes	(no)	_tomorrow morning_
2. ❏ magazine			
❏ perishable item			
❏ large envelope	yes	no	_____
3. ❏ parcel			
❏ perishable item			
❏ letter	yes	no	_____
4. ❏ large envelope			
❏ magazine			
❏ parcel	yes	no	_____
5. ❏ perishable item			
❏ parcel			
❏ large envelope	yes	no	_____

11. Before Ken moved to his new apartment, he filled out this change of address card and mailed it to the post office. Read the card. Ask your teacher if you don't understand.

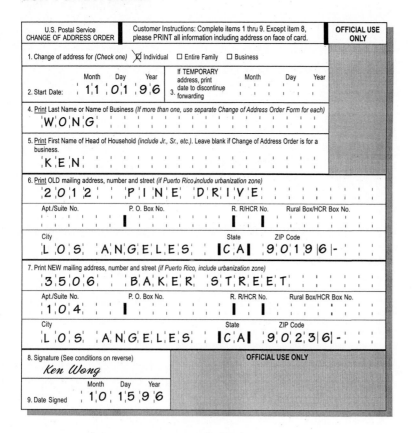

Notes:

1. **People with different last names cannot use the same change of address card.**

2. **When you go on vacation, you can ask the post office to hold your mail until you come back.**

12. Write answers to the questions.

1. How many people moved?

_____

2. When did Ken move?

_____

3. Was the move temporary or permanent?

_____

4. Before he moved, where did Ken live?

_____

5. Where did he move to?

_____

 In your country, what happens if the mail carrier brings a parcel to your house and no one is home?

Did You Go Shopping Last Weekend?

1. Look at the pictures. Answer your teacher's questions. (Teacher, see page 208.)

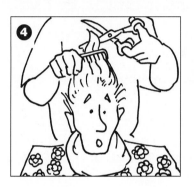

Topic: weekend activities
Life skill: returning/exchanging clothing
Structure: past tense

Weekend Activities

2. Learn the new words. Listen to the words. Repeat them after your teacher.

① go shopping **②** see friends **③** eat out **④** get a haircut

⑤ have fun **⑥** come home late **⑦** meet someone new **⑧** sleep late

⑨ leave the city **⑩** write a letter **⑪** speak English **⑫** tell a lie

PAIRWORK. Practice with a partner. Student A, look at this page and say the words. Student B, look at page 129 and point to the pictures.

Conversation

3. Practice the conversation with your teacher.

A: Did you go shopping last weekend?
B: Yes, I did. Did you?
A: No, I didn't.

A: Did you leave the city last weekend?
B: No, I didn't. Did you?
A: Yes, I did.

PAIRWORK. Now look at page 129. Make new conversations with your partner.

Last Weekend

Irregular verbs do not use -ed.

4. Listen to the examples below. Repeat them after your teacher.

1. come ➡ came
2. eat ➡ ate
3. get ➡ got
4. go ➡ went

5. have ➡ had
6. leave ➡ left
7. meet ➡ met
8. see ➡ saw

9. sleep ➡ slept
10. speak ➡ spoke
11. tell ➡ told
12. write ➡ wrote

I **went** shopping last weekend. I **ate** out last weekend.	I **didn't go** shopping last weekend. I **didn't eat** out last weekend.

PAIRWORK. Look at the pictures on page 129.
Tell a partner what you did and didn't do last weekend.

Writing Practice

5. Write sentences about your weekend. (Write about the pictures on page 129.)

Examples: I went shopping last weekend.

          I didn't eat out last weekend.

1. _____
2. _____
3. _____
4. _____
5. _____
6. _____
7. _____
8. _____
9. _____
10. _____

6. Below are some more irregular verbs. Talk with your classmates and teacher. Think of words to come next and write them.

1. buy ➡ bought
   new clothes
   _____
   _____
   _____

2. do ➡ did
   _____
   _____
   _____
   _____

3. drink ➡ drank
   _____
   _____
   _____
   _____

4. feel ➡ felt
   a little sad
   _____
   _____
   _____

5. make ➡ made
   _____
   _____
   _____
   _____

6. ride ➡ rode
   my bicycle
   _____
   _____
   _____

7. take ➡ took
   _____
   _____
   _____
   _____

8. wear ➡ wore
   _____
   _____
   _____
   _____

Now use your ideas to write sentences.

Examples: I rode my bicycle to school yesterday.

             I didn't buy any new clothes last weekend.

1. _____

2. _____

3. _____

4. _____

5. _____

6. _____

7. _____

Returns and Exchanges

7. Judy is at a department store. Listen to her conversations with the salesclerks. Then practice them with your teacher.

1. **Salesclerk:** Hello. May I help you?
    Judy: Yes. I bought this shirt for my boyfriend, but it's too small.
    Salesclerk: What size is it?
    Judy: It's a medium.
    Salesclerk: Do you want to return it or exchange it for a large?
    Judy: I'd like to exchange it, please. Here's the receipt.
    Salesclerk: And here's the shirt in a large.
    Judy: Thank you.

2. **Salesclerk:** Hello. May I help you?
    Judy: Yes. I bought these shoes for my niece, but they're too big.
    Salesclerk: What size are they?
    Judy: They're size five.
    Salesclerk: Do you want to return them or exchange them for size four?
    Judy: I'd like to return them, please. Here's the receipt.
    Salesclerk: And here's your money—$17.69.
    Judy: Thank you.

8. Listen to other conversations at the department store. Circle the problem with the clothing. Then check (✔) *return* or *exchange* and write what the customer gets.

Problem	Return or exchange?	What does the customer get?
1. (too big) / too small	❑ return / ☑ exchange	coat–size 12
2. too big / too small	❑ return / ❑ exchange	
3. too big / too small	❑ return / ❑ exchange	
4. too big / too small	❑ return / ❑ exchange	
5. too big / too small	❑ return / ❑ exchange	

Returns and Exchanges

9. **Listen to the conversation and write the missing words. Then practice it with a partner.**

Salesclerk: Hello. May I help you?

Customer: Yes. I bought this _____ for my _____,

but it's too _____.

Salesclerk: What size is it?

Customer: It's size _____.

Salesclerk: Do you want to return it or exchange it for a size _____?

Customer: I'd like to _____ it, please.

Here's the receipt.

Salesclerk: Oh, I'm sorry. This _____ was on sale. You can't return it,

but you can _____ it for something else.

Customer: I see. Then maybe I'll look for a _____.

10. **Write the names of clothing you might buy for family or friends.**

1. _sweater_____   6. _____

2. _____   7. _____

3. _____   8. _____

4. _____   9. _____

5. _____   10. _____

With your partner, make new conversations about returning and exchanging the clothing above. Take turns being the customer and the salesclerk.

In your country, what do you do if you buy something that is too big or too small?

134   Unit 21

What Happened to Judy?

1. Look at the pictures. Answer your teacher's questions. (Teacher, see page 208.)

Judy

Joe

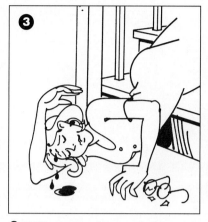

Susan

Linda

Mr. Sato

Paul

Mrs. Sato

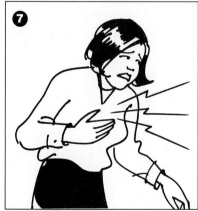

Carlos

Ken

Topic: accidents and emergencies
Life skill: calling Emergency 911
Structure: past tense

2. Learn the new words. Listen to the sentences. Repeat them after your teacher.

	WHAT HAPPENED	WHAT TO DO

WHAT HAPPENED

A dog bit her.

Her hand is bleeding.

    bite ➡ bit

WHAT TO DO

Wash her hand well.

Put a bandage on her hand.

Call 911. Watch the dog!

A car hit him.

He's unconscious.

    hit ➡ hit

Call 911.

> **Same meaning**
> ___
> **She's unconscious.**
> **She passed out.**

She fell down.

She cut her head.

    fall ➡ fell

    cut ➡ cut

Take her to the emergency room
if the cut is deep.

Call 911 if she's unconscious.

She got an electric shock.

Call 911 if she's unconscious.

He's choking.

(He can't breathe.)

Let him cough.

Help him if you know how.

He drank medicine.

(He drank poison.)

Call 911.

(continued on next page)

Accidents and Emergencies

	WHAT HAPPENED	**WHAT TO DO**
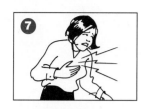	She's having chest pains.	Tell her to sit down. Call the doctor. Call 911 if she passes out.
	He burned his hand.	Put ice on his hand.
	He stepped on a nail.	Wash the cut well.

PAIRWORK. Practice with a partner. Student A, look at pages 136 and 137 and say what happened. Student B, look at page 135 and point to the pictures.

Listen and Write

3. **Listen and complete the sentences.**

1. Quick! Get a bandage. Susan _____ _____ and cut her head!

2. Oh, no! Poor Linda got an _____ shock!

3. Please help! Mr. Sato can't breathe! _____ _____.

4. Call 911! Joe was crossing the street and a _____ _____ him.

5. Hurry! Get some ice. Carlos _____ his hand.

6. Quick! Stop Paul! He's drinking _____.

7. Get a bandage. Judy's hand _____ _____.

8. Mrs. Sato is having _____ _____. Call the doctor.

9. Get water to wash Ken's foot. He _____ on a nail.

10. Quick! Call 911. Susan is on the floor. She _____ _____.

4. Listen and write the number of each conversation under the correct picture.

A

B

C

D

E

F

1   Judy

G

H

I

Now listen again and write each person's name beside the number.

Conversation

5. Practice the conversations with your teacher.

A: Quick! Help!
B: What happened?
A: Carlos burned his hand.
B: What should we do?
A: Let's put some ice on his hand.
B: OK. I'll do it.

A: Quick! Help!
B: What's the matter?
A: A dog bit Judy's hand.
B: What should we do?
A: Let's wash her hand and put a bandage on it.
B: OK. I'll do it.

PAIRWORK. Now look at page 135. Make new conversations with a partner.

911 Emergency

6. Learn the new words. Look at the pictures and repeat the words after your teacher.

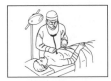
ambulance

emergency room

fire truck

police car

Listen to Susan's conversation with the 911 operator. Then practice it with your teacher.

Operator: 911 Emergency.
Susan: Hello. I need help. My son just drank some cough medicine.
Operator: What kind did he drink?
Susan: Phenergan.
Operator: How much did he drink?
Susan: The **whole bottle.**
Operator: What's your address?
Susan: 1029 Twenty-second Street.
Operator: Do you have a car?
Susan: Yes, I do.
Operator: Then take your son to the emergency room at Mercy Hospital. The address is 586 Austin Avenue.
Susan: Thank you. Good-bye.

7. Listen to the conversations and write the number of each conversation under the correct picture. Then write what's coming: an ambulance, a fire truck, or a police car.

_____ _____ _____ _____

What's coming?   What's coming?   What's coming?   What's coming?

_____ _____ _____ _____

What Happened to Judy? 139

8. Read about emergency phone calls. Ask your teacher if you don't understand.

> **Dial 911 for the police, the fire department, an ambulance, or poison control.**

Things you can say:	Things they might say:
1. Someone is trying to get into my apartment.	a. Stay on the line.
2. There's a car accident on the corner of _____ and _____. Someone is **hurt.**	b. Don't move him. c. Keep him quiet.
3. My mother is unconscious.	d. Cover her with a blanket. e. Keep her warm.
4. My son drank poison.	f. Give him a glass of water. g. Make him vomit. h. Take him to the emergency room.
5. There's a fire at _____.	i. We'll send a fire truck.

9. Before you listen to each speaker, read the sentences with your teacher. Then listen to the speaker and circle the letter of what to say next.

1. a. Make him vomit.
   b. We'll send a fire truck.
   c. Don't move him. *(circled)*

2. a. Yes, he is.
   b. A dog bit him.
   c. No, he didn't.

3. a. Cover him with a blanket.
   b. Wash his hand well.
   c. Give him a glass of water.

4. a. Chest pains.
   b. Half a cup.
   c. An electric shock.

5. a. Stay on the line.
   b. There was a car accident.
   c. Let him cough.

6. a. Tell her to sit down.
   b. Yes. The drivers are unconscious.
   c. Wash her hand well.

7. a. Take him to the emergency room.
   b. Is anyone hurt?
   c. What's your neighbor's address?

8. a. I don't know.
   b. He's choking.
   c. Stay on the line.

9. a. Don't move.
   b. Are they unconscious?
   c. What's your address?

10. a. Cover her with a blanket.
    b. Make her vomit.
    c. We'll send a police officer.

911 Emergency

10. **Look at the picture and complete the conversation. Then practice it with a partner.**

Operator: 911 Emergency.

You: Hello. I need help. _____

_____ .

Operator: Is _____ unconscious?

You: _____ .

Operator: What's your name?

You: _____ .

Operator: What's your address?

You: _____ .

Operator: OK. Don't _____ .

Keep _____ .

We'll send _____ right
away.

You: Thank you. Good-bye.

11. **Complete the story about what happened above. Use the past tense
of the verbs in the box.**

be	call	come	fall	feel	take	tell

Yesterday, my _____ *fell* _____ down the stairs. _____

_____ unconscious, and I _____ scared. First, I

_____ 911. Then I _____ the operator my name

and address. Ten minutes later, the ambulance _____ to our house.

Finally, the ambulance _____ my _____ to the hospital.

How do people report emergencies in your country?

12. With a partner, write a conversation about a fire, a car accident, a medical emergency, or someone trying to get inside a house or apartment. Then practice the conversation with your partner.

Operator: 911 Emergency.

You: Hello. I need help.

_____ .

Operator: _____ ?

You: _____ .

Operator: _____ ?

You: _____ .

Operator: _____ ?

You: _____ .

Operator: OK. _____ .

_____ .

You: Thank you. Good-bye.

13. Write a story about what happened above.

Yesterday, _____

_____

_____

_____

_____

_____

Now close your book and tell your story to the class.

Where Did Carlos Have His Checkup?

1. Look at the pictures. Answer your teacher's questions. (Teacher, see page 208.)

	FRIDAY	**SATURDAY**

Topic: health matters
Life skill: medical checkup
Structure: past tense

Trying to Stay Healthy

2. Learn the new words. Read the sentences. Repeat them after your teacher.

 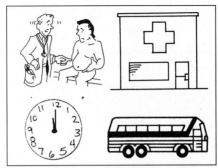 

1. On Friday, Carlos had a checkup at the clinic at noon. He got there by bus.
2. On Saturday, he went jogging in the park in the morning. He ran five miles.

3. On Friday, Judy played tennis with Ken after work. They walked to the playground.
4. On Saturday, she watched TV at home with her dog because her feet were sore.

5. On Friday, the parrot talked all day to the cat. He spoke three languages.
6. On Saturday, he drank lemon and honey tea because he had a sore throat.
   He drank seven cups.

PAIRWORK. Now look at page 143. Make sentences with a partner.

Conversation

Wh _____	did	he she it	_____ ?

3. Practice the conversations with your teacher.

1.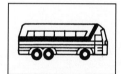

   A: What did Carlos do on Friday?
   B: He had a checkup.

2.

   A: Where did he have the checkup?
   B: At the clinic.

3.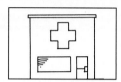

   A: How did he **get** to the clinic?
   B: By bus.

4.

   A: How many miles did he run on Saturday?
   B: Five miles.

5.

   A: When did Judy play tennis?
   B: After work.

6.

   A: Who did she play tennis **with**?
   B: Ken.

7.

   A: Why did she watch TV on Saturday?
   B: Because her feet were sore.

PAIRWORK. Now look at page 143. Make new conversations with a partner.

Learn about Your Classmates

| Wh _____ did you _____ ? |

4. **Practice the conversation with your teacher.**

A: What did you do last weekend?
B: I saw a movie.

A: What movie did you see?
B: *The Long Summer.*

A: Where did you see it?
B: At a theater near my house.

A: When did you go?
B: Saturday afternoon.

A: Who did you go with?
B: My husband and kids.

A: How did you get to the theater?
B: We walked there.

A: Did you have a good time?
B: Pretty good. It was a funny movie.

PAIRWORK. Now close your book and ask two classmates about last weekend or last summer. Ask: 1. *What?* 2. *Where?* 3. *When?* 4. *Who...with?* and 5. *How?*

After you finish talking, write about your classmates' weekend or summer.

Example: _José played soccer with his friends on Saturday._

1. _____

2. _____

3. _____

4. _____

5. _____

Body Parts and Organs

5. Look at the words and repeat them after your teacher. Then write the words on the correct lines on the body.

1. head	15. stomach
2. face	16. arm
3. forehead	17. elbow
4. eye	18. wrist
5. nose	19. hand
6. mouth	20. finger
7. lip	21. thumb
8. chin	22. hip
9. cheek	23. leg
10. ear	24. knee
11. neck	25. ankle
12. shoulder	26. foot
13. back	27. heel
14. chest	28. toe

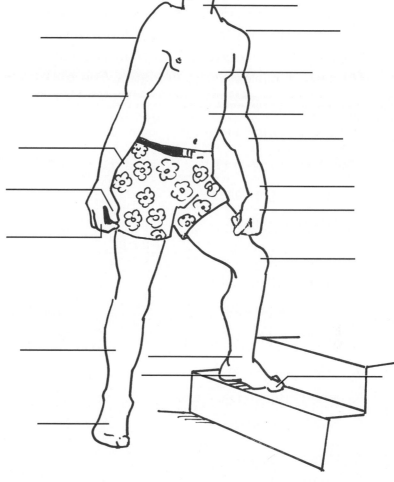

6. Learn the new words. These organs are *inside* the body. Look at the pictures and repeat the words after your teacher.

heart	lungs	kidneys	intestine	liver

Now draw a line from each organ to the correct place in the body above.

A Medical Checkup

7. Learn the new words. Look at the words and repeat them after your teacher.

breathe urinate	nauseous congested

8. Carlos is at the doctor's office. Listen to his conversation with the doctor. Then practice it with your teacher.

Doctor: How are you, Carlos?
Carlos: Not so good. It hurts when I urinate.
Doctor: Hmm. When did this problem start?
Carlos: Four days **ago**. What can I do about it?
Doctor: First, we'll do some **tests**. You **may** have a kidney infection.

9. Listen to other people talking to the doctor. Circle the problem each person has. Then write when it started.

What's the problem?	When did it start?	Do tests?	Doctor's diagnosis
1. Her eyes are yellow.			⟮lung infection⟯
It hurts to urinate.		☐ yes	liver problem
⟮She's congested.⟯	__1 week__ ago	☑ no	kidney infection
2. She has diarrhea.			heart problem
She can't breathe.		☐ yes	intestinal infection
She's nauseous.	_____ ago	☐ no	lung infection
3. She's congested.			kidney infection
It hurts to urinate.		☐ yes	intestinal infection
She has a cough.	_____ ago	☐ no	heart problem
4. He's run-down.			heart problem
He has diarrhea.		☐ yes	liver problem
His eyes are yellow.	_____ ago	☐ no	intestinal infection
5. He has a fever.			lung infection
He can't breathe.		☐ yes	heart problem
He's nauseous.	_____ ago	☐ no	intestinal infection

Listen again. Check (✔) *yes* if the people are going to have tests and check *no* if they aren't. Then circle the doctor's diagnosis.

10. The sentences in this conversation are not in the correct order. Number the sentences correctly and write the conversation below. Then practice it with a partner.

_____ First, we'll do some tests.

_____ Not so good. I have diarrhea.

___1___ How are you?

_____ Five days ago.

_____ You may have an infection in your intestine.

_____ Hmm. When did this problem start?

_____ What can I do about it?

Doctor: _____

Patient: _____

Doctor: _____

Patient: _____

_____

Doctor: _____

_____

11. You are having a checkup. Complete the conversation about a medical problem you have. Then practice it with your partner.

Doctor: How are you, _____

You: Not so good. _____

Doctor: Hmm. When did this problem start?

You: _____

What can I _____

Doctor: First, _____

You may have _____

How often do people have medical checkups in your country?

Your Medical History

12. **Fill out the medical history form.**

PATIENT INFORMATION

Please print all information.

Name _____
          (Last)   (First)   (M.I.)

Address _____ Telephone No. _____

Birthdate _____ Age _____
                    mo./day/yr.

Sex M ☐   F ☐   Soc. Sec. No._____

Insurance? Yes ☐ No ☐   If yes, name of company _____

Marital Status   Married ☐   Single ☐   Children?   Yes ☐   No ☐

Do you take any medication regularly?   Yes ☐   No ☐

         If yes, name of medication _____

Date of last medical checkup _____

Check the problems you have:

         ☐ Headache   ☐ Heart problems

         ☐ Backache   ☐ Intestinal problems

         ☐ Chest pain   ☐ Kidney problems

         ☐ Stomachache   ☐ Liver problems

         ☐ Diarrhea   ☐ Lung problems

         ☐ Allergies

              What are you allergic to? _____

In case of emergency, contact   (name) _____

                                      (telephone #) _____

Yesterday, Today, and Tomorrow

1. Look at the pictures. Answer your teacher's questions. **(Teacher, see page 209.)**

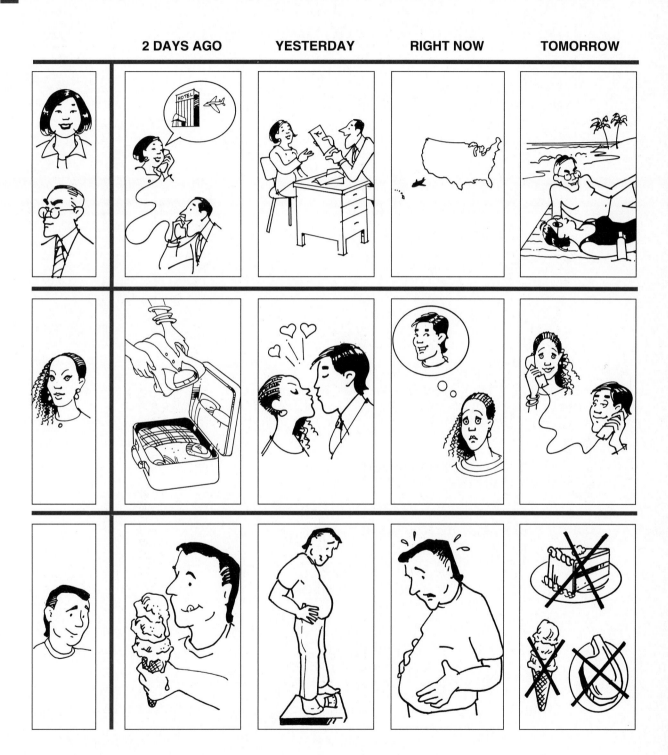

Topic: travel
Life skill: making reservations
Structure: tense review

151

Summertime Ups and Downs

2. Learn the new words. Listen to the words. Repeat them after your teacher.

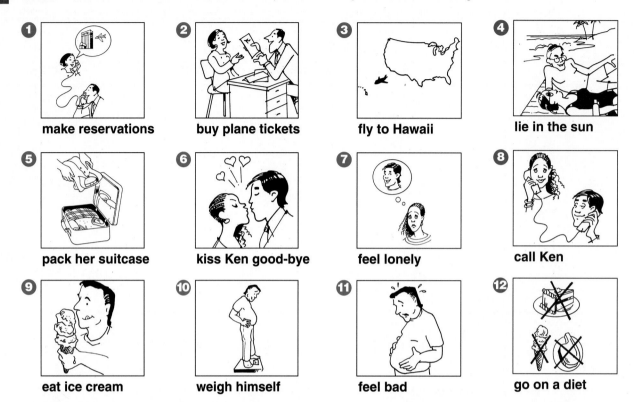

1. make reservations
2. buy plane tickets
3. fly to Hawaii
4. lie in the sun
5. pack her suitcase
6. kiss Ken good-bye
7. feel lonely
8. call Ken
9. eat ice cream
10. weigh himself
11. feel bad
12. go on a diet

PAIRWORK. Practice with a partner. Student A, look at this page and say the words. Student B, look at page 151 and point to the pictures.

Listen and Write

3. Listen and complete the sentences.

1. Yesterday the Satos _____ _____ _____ for their trip.

2. Judy is _____ _____ right now.

3. Carlos _____ _____ yesterday.

4. Tomorrow the Satos are going to _____ _____ _____ _____ .

5. Two days ago, Judy_____ _____ _____ .

6. The Satos_____ _____ for their trip two days ago.

7. Carlos is going to _____ _____ _____ _____ tomorrow.

8. Right now the Satos _____ _____ to Hawaii.

Conversation

4. Practice the conversations with your teacher.

1.
   A: What **did** the Satos do two days ago?
   B: They made reservations for their trip.

2.
   A: What **did** they do yesterday?
   B: They bought their plane tickets.

3.
   A: What are they do**ing** right now?
   B: Flying to Hawaii.

4.
   A: What are they **going to** do tomorrow?
   B: Lie in the sun.

5.
   A: What did Judy do two days ago?
   B: She packed her suitcase.

6.
   A: What did she do yesterday?
   B: She kissed Ken good-bye.

7.
   A: What is she doing right now?
   B: Feeling lonely.

8.
   A: What is she going to do tomorrow?
   B: Call Ken.

PAIRWORK. Now look at page 151. Make conversations with a partner.

Already/Not Yet

Did you already _____?	Yes,	I did.
	No,	I didn't not yet.

5. Practice the conversations with your teacher.

A: How often do you read the newspaper?
B: Every day.
A: Did you already read the newspaper today?
B: Yes, I did.
A: When did you read it?
B: At breakfast time.

A: How often do you write to your mother?
B: Every week.
A: Did you already write to her this week?
B: No, not yet.
A: When are you going to write to her?
B: On Sunday.

PAIRWORK. Close your book and make new conversations with a partner. Ask three questions: 1. *How often?* 2. *Already?* and 3. *When?* Ask about these things. (Teacher, write the cues on the chalkboard for the students' pair practice.)

clean the house   **go shopping**   **take a shower**   **do the laundry**   **kiss your husband/wife**

I already _____ .	I didn't _____ yet.

6. Write sentences about yourself.

Examples: ___I already took a shower today.___

___I didn't eat lunch yet.___

1. _____

2. _____

3. _____

7. Mrs. Sato is making an airline reservation. Listen to her conversation with the travel agent. Then practice it with your teacher.

Mrs. Sato:	Hello. I'd like to make a plane reservation to Hawaii.
Travel agent:	Your name, please?
Mrs. Sato:	Kitty Sato
Travel agent:	How many are in your **party?**
Mrs. Sato:	Two. My husband and me.
Travel agent:	When do you want to leave?
Mrs. Sato:	July 25th.
Travel agent:	And when do you want to return?
Mrs. Sato:	August 2nd.
Travel agent:	All right. On July 25th, Flight 258 on World Airlines leaves Los Angeles at 11:45. A.M. and arrives in Hawaii at 1:30 P.M. Is that OK?
Mrs. Sato:	Leave 11:45. Arrive 1:30. Yes, that's OK.
Travel agent:	On August 2nd, Flight 710 leaves Hawaii at 9:00 A.M. and arrives in Los Angeles at 6:45 P.M. OK?
Mrs. Sato:	Leave 9:00. Arrive 6:45. Yes, that's OK.
Travel agent:	All right, Mrs. Sato. I'll have your tickets ready in a few minutes.

8. Listen to other people making airline reservations. Write the number of people in each party. Then write the dates and times of **departure** and **arrival** for each flight.

Number in party		Date	Departure time	Arrival time
1. ___1___	**Leave:**	Dec. 22	8:15 A.M.	2:20 P.M.
	Return:	_____	_____	_____
2. _____	**Leave:**	_____	_____	_____
	Return:	_____	_____	_____
3. _____	**Leave:**	_____	_____	_____
	Return:	_____	_____	_____
4. _____	**Leave:**	_____	_____	_____
	Return:	_____	_____	_____
5. _____	**Leave:**	_____	_____	_____
	Return:	_____	_____	_____

Airline Reservations

9. Complete the conversation with information about an airline reservation you'd like to make. Then practice it with a partner.

You: Hello. I'd like to make a plane reservation to _____.

Agent: Your name, please?

You: _____.

Agent: When do you want to leave?

You: _____.

Agent: And when do you want to return?

You: _____.

Agent: All right. On _____, Flight 258 on World Airlines leaves _____

at _____ and arrives in _____ at _____. OK?

You: _____.

Agent: All right. I'll have your ticket ready in a few minutes.

Arrivals and Departures

10. Read about flight arrivals and departures. Then write answers to the questions.

ARRIVALS				DEPARTURES			
From	*Flight #*	*Gate*	*Time*	*To*	*Flight #*	*Gate*	*Time*
Boston	986	66	11:00 A.M.	Boston	1808	9	11:45 A.M.
Chicago	1057	5	12:30 P.M.	Chicago	629	80	2:00 P.M.
Houston	1224	10	10:10 A.M.	Houston	356	25	11:50 A.M.
Seattle	492	49	1:25 P.M.	Seattle	702	3	3:15 P.M.

1. When is the plane from Houston going to arrive? _____

2. What is the flight number of the plane coming from Chicago? _____

3. What gate will Flight 702 leave from? _____

4. When is the plane to Chicago going to leave? _____

Where do people like to travel in your country?

What Should I Do Next?

1. Look at the pictures. Answer your teacher's questions. **(Teacher, see page 209.)**

2 lbs.

1 doz.

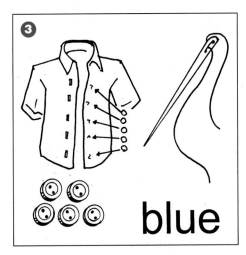

blue

white

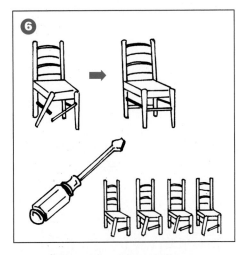

Topic: job responsibilities
Life skills: requesting instructions;
**   job benefits**
Structure: modal *should* in questions

ob Duties

2. Learn the new words. Listen to the sentences. Repeat them after your teacher.

①

Peel apples.
Use a knife.
Peel two pounds.

②

Make boxes.
Use glue.
Make one dozen.

③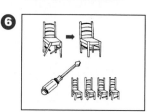

Sew buttons.
Use a needle and thread.
Sew five buttons.
Use blue thread.

④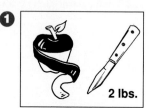

Paint the walls.
Use a paintbrush.
Paint the whole room.
Use white paint.

⑤

Wash windows.
Use a sponge.
Do the whole house.

⑥

Fix chairs.
Use a screwdriver.
Fix four chairs.

PAIRWORK. Practice with a partner. Student A, look at this page and say the words.
Student B, look at page 157 and point to the pictures.

isten and Write

3. Listen and complete the sentences.

1. I want you to _____ these _____ .

2. Please use a _____ to wash the windows.

3. I want you to _____ those _____ now.

4. Use glue to _____ those _____ .

5. Could you please paint the _____ ?

6. I want you to use _____ thread on those _____ , OK?

7. Would you please make _____ boxes?

8. I want you to use a _____ on those _____ .

Conversation

| Wh_____should I _____? |

4. **Listen to the workers ask for instructions.** Then practice the conversations with your teacher.

1. **Worker:** What should I do next?
   Supervisor: I want you to peel apples.

2. **2 lbs.** **Worker:** How many apples should I peel?
   Supervisor: Two pounds.

3. **Worker:** What should I use to peel them?
   Supervisor: Use a knife.

   Worker: Got it!

4. **Worker:** What should I do next?
   Supervisor: I want you to paint the walls.

5. **Worker:** How many walls should I paint?
   Supervisor: The whole room.

6. **white** **Worker:** What color paint should I use?
   Supervisor: White.

   Worker: Got it!

PAIRWORK. Now look at page 157. Make new conversations with a partner. Take turns being the worker and supervisor.

Writing Practice

5. Write a conversation between a worker and a supervisor where *you* work.

Worker: _____

Supervisor: I want you to _____

Worker: _____

Supervisor: _____

Worker: _____

Supervisor: Use _____

Worker: _____

6. Look at the pictures. Answer your teacher's questions. **(Teacher, see page 210.)**

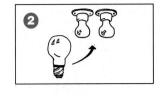

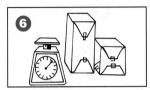

Now look at the bottom of this page. Repeat the sentences in the box after your teacher.

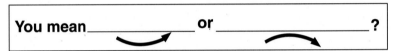

You mean _____ or _____ ?

7. Practice the conversations with your teacher.

Supervisor:	Would you wipe that cabinet?
Worker:	You mean the inside or the outside?
Supervisor:	The outside.
Worker:	Got it.
Supervisor:	Let me know when you're finished, OK?
Worker:	OK.

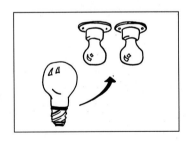

Supervisor:	Would you change that light bulb?
Worker:	You mean the left one or the right one?
Supervisor:	The left one.
Worker:	Got it.
Supervisor:	Let me know when you're through, OK?
Worker:	OK.

Same meaning: finished = through = done

PAIRWORK. Now cover the bottom half of this page and make new conversations with a partner. Take turns being the worker and supervisor. The supervisor can give any answer.

1. Wipe the cabinet.	2. Change the lightbulb.	3. Sweep the restroom.
4. Put this in the drawer.	5. Empty the wastebasket.	6. Weigh the package.

Understanding Pay Stubs

7. This pay stub came with Ken's paycheck this **pay period.** Read the pay stub with a partner. Ask your teacher if you don't understand. Then write answers to the questions below.

Name: Ken Wong   616-08-9532

Regular Hours	Overtime Hours	Regular Pay	Overtime Pay	Gross Pay	Period Ending
80	8	600.00	80.00	680.00	3/15/96

Deductions This Pay Period

Fed. With. Tax	F.I.C.A.	State Tax	Insurance	Union Dues
102.00	47.60	15.09	30.00	00.00

Gross Pay	Net Pay
680.00	485.31

Earnings This Pay Period

Gross Pay	Fed. Tax	F.I.C.A.	State Tax	Insurance	Union Dues
3,400.00	510.00	238.00	75.45	150.00	00.00

Year-To-Date Totals

---

1. What was the last day of the pay period? _____

2. How many regular hours did Ken work? _____

3. What was his regular pay? _____

4. How many overtime hours did Ken work? _____

5. What was his gross pay? _____

6. What **deductions** did Ken have? _____

7. How much did he pay in taxes? _____

8. How much insurance did he pay? _____

9. What was Ken's **take-home pay** (net pay)? _____

10. What is Ken's gross pay for the year so far? _____

Understanding Pay Stubs

8. Read about how paychecks are figured. Ask your teacher if you don't understand.

Regular pay	=	regular hours	x	regular hourly pay rate
Overtime pay	=	overtime hours	x	overtime hourly pay rate
Gross pay	=	regular pay	+	overtime pay
Take-home pay	=	gross pay	–	deductions

9. Read about Carlos. Then work with a partner and write answers to the questions below.

Carlos worked forty hours this week at $16.00 an hour. He worked six hours overtime at $24.00 an hour. Here are his deductions for the week.

Federal tax	$94.08	F.I.C.A.	$54.88
State tax	$18.62	Union dues	$12.00

1. What is Carlos's regular pay? _____

2. What is Carlos's overtime pay? _____

3. What is Carlos's gross pay? _____

4. What are Carlos's **total** deductions? _____

5. What is Carlos's take-home pay? _____

10. Look at one of your own pay stubs. If you don't have a job, get a pay stub from a family member, a friend, or your teacher. Answer the questions.

1. What pay period is the check for? _____

2. How many hours did you work? _____

3. What was your gross pay? _____

4. What deductions did you have?   Amount?

    a. _____   _____

    b. _____   _____

    c. _____   _____

    d. _____   _____

5. What was your take-home pay? _____

 In your country, are taxes deducted from people's pay?

Is Your Hometown Rainy?

1. Look at the pictures. Answer your teacher's questions. (Teacher, see page 210.)

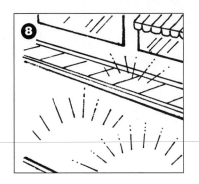

Topic: your hometown
Life skill: invitations
Structure: comparatives

Describing Places

2. Learn the new words. Listen to the words. Repeat them after your teacher.

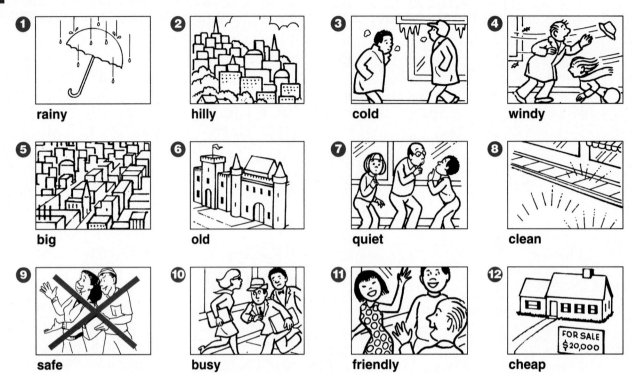

1. rainy
2. hilly
3. cold
4. windy
5. big
6. old
7. quiet
8. clean
9. safe
10. busy
11. friendly
12. cheap

PAIRWORK. Practice with a partner. Student A, look at this page and say the words. Student B, look at page 169 and point to the pictures.

Listen and Write

3. Listen and complete the sentences.

1. I like walking on the streets because they're so _____.

2. The downtown part of my hometown is really_____.

3. I like the people there because they are _____.

4. You have to hold on to your hat because it's often _____ !

5. Everyone carries umbrellas there because it's so _____.

6. You get tired walking there because the town is_____.

7. It's OK to walk there at night because it's _____.

8. There's no problem sleeping there because it's always_____.

omparing

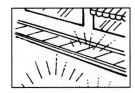

Which is _____**er, your hometown or this city?**

4. Practice the conversation with your teacher.

A: Which is cleaner, your hometown or this city?
B: My hometown.

A: Which is colder, your hometown or this city?
B: This city.

A: Which is safer, your hometown or this city?
B: They're about the same.

PAIRWORK. Now look at page 169. Make new conversations with a partner.

Spelling

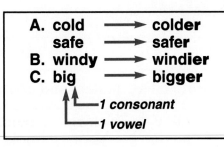

A. cold ⟶ colder
   safe ⟶ safer
B. windy ⟶ windier
C. big ⟶ bigger
   1 consonant
   1 vowel

Irregular words

good ⟶ better
bad ⟶ worse
far ⟶ farther/further

5. Add _-er_ to these words. Follow the examples above.

1. happy _____
2. sad _____
3. hilly _____
4. clean _____
5. rainy _____

6. old _____
7. cheap _____
8. friendly _____
9. hot _____
10. nice _____

11. early _____
12. fast _____
13. flat _____
14. busy _____
15. tall _____

Learn about Your Classmates

Is your hometown _____ er than this city?

6. Practice the conversation with your teacher.

    A: Where are you from?
    B: I'm from Shanghai. How about you?
    A: I'm from Tijuana.

    A: Is Shanghai older than this city?
    B: Yes, it is.

    A: Is Shanghai bigger than this city?
    B: No, it isn't.

    A: Is Shanghai quieter than this city?
    B: They're about the same.

PAIRWORK. Look at page 169. Make new conversations with a partner. Compare your hometowns and the city where you live now.

Writing Practice

_____ is _____ er than _____ .

7. Write sentences comparing cities, states, and countries. Use words from the box.

large	cold	rainy	clean	quiet	flat	busy
small	hot	sunny	poor	noisy	hilly	friendly

Examples: New York is colder than California.

               China is larger than Mexico.

1. _____
2. _____
3. _____
4. _____
5. _____

8. Look at the pictures. Answer your teacher's questions. (Teacher, see page 211.)

Now look at the bottom of this page. Repeat the words in the box after your teacher.

Which do you like	better, more,	_____ ing or _____ ing?

9. Practice the conversation with your teacher.

A: Which do you like better, eating out or eating at home?
B: Eating out. How about you?
A: Me too.

A: Which do you like more, walking or taking the bus?
B: Walking. What about you?
A: I like taking the bus.

A: Which do you like better, reading or watching TV?
B: I like them about the same.

PAIRWORK. Now cover the bottom half of this page and make new conversations with a partner.

1. **live in the city / live in the country**	4. **get up early / sleep late**
2. **walk / take the bus**	5. **read / watch TV**
3. **eat out / eat at home**	6. **go out / stay home**

Invitations

10. Susan and Carlos are inviting friends to do things this weekend. Listen to their conversations and write the missing words. Then practice the conversations with your teacher.

1. **Susan:** Say, Betsy, would you like to ____ _____ with me this weekend?

   Betsy: Sure. **I'd love to.**

   Susan: Great. Which day is _____ for you, Saturday or Sunday?

   Betsy: _____ is better for me.

   Susan: OK.

   Betsy: What time _____ we go?

   Susan: How about_____?

   Betsy: That sounds fine. **I'll look forward to it.**

2. **Carlos:** Say, Tom, would you and Marsha like to _____ _____ for dinner this weekend?

   Tom: We'd love to, but we _____.

   This weekend we're _____ out of town.

   Carlos: Oh, well. Maybe some other time.

   Tom: Yeah. Thanks anyway.

11. Take turns inviting a partner to do things this weekend. Use the pictures below and the conversations above.

 What kinds of things do people invite their friends to do in your country?

UNIT 28 Is Your Hometown Crowded?

1. Look at the pictures. Answer your teacher's questions. (Teacher, see page 211.)

FOR SALE
$300,000

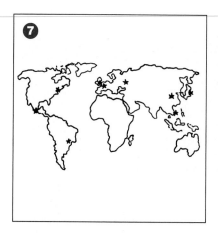

Topic: your hometown
Life skill: compliments
Structure: comparatives

175

2. Learn the new words. Listen to the words. Repeat them after your teacher.

① crowded

② beautiful

③ modern

④ expensive
FOR SALE $300,000

⑤ dangerous

⑥ scenic

⑦ famous

⑧ interesting

⑨ fun

PAIRWORK. Practice with a partner. Student A, look at this page and say the words. Student B, look at page 175 and point to the pictures.

Listen and Write

3. Listen and complete the sentences.

1. Everyone takes pictures there because it's so _____.

2. I don't like to take the buses there. They're too_____.

3. The museums in my hometown are really_____.

4. I don't like walking there at night because it's _____!

5. Everybody knows about my city. It's very _____.

6. All the buildings in my hometown are new. It's a _____ city.

7. You have to be rich to live here because it's so _____.

8. There are lots of places to eat out or go dancing. It's a _____ city.

Which is	safer, rainier, **more** crowded, **more** scenic,	your hometown or this city?

4. Practice the conversation with your teacher.

A: Which is more scenic, your hometown or this city?
B: My hometown.

A: Which is more crowded, your hometown or this city?
B: They're about the same.

PAIRWORK. Now look at page 175. Make new conversations with a partner.

Writing Practice

_____ is **more** _____ than _____ .

5. Write sentences comparing cities, states, and countries.

Examples: __The United States is more expensive than Mexico.__

__Beijing is more famous than Podunk City.__

1. _____
2. _____
3. _____
4. _____
5. _____
6. _____

Giving Compliments

6. Susan is visiting the Satos in their new apartment. Listen to the conversation. Then practice it with your teacher.

Susan: I really like your new apartment.
Mrs. Sato: Thank you.
Susan: It's so sunny. Is it quiet?
Mrs. Sato: Yes, it is. This apartment is quieter than our old one.

7. Listen to other people giving compliments. Circle what they are talking about. Then write how it is different from the old one.

What is it?			How is it different?
1. garage	(house)	basement	It's bigger.
2. bathroom	bedroom	kitchen	_____
3. sweater	coat	jacket	_____
4. bicycle	motorcycle	car	_____
5. boyfriend	neighbor	roommate	_____

8. With your teacher, think of words to talk about clothes. Write the words in the spaces below.

1. pretty   4. _____   7. _____

2. warm   5. _____   8. _____

3. comfortable   6. _____   9. _____

Work with a partner. Take turns giving compliments about your partner's clothes.

In your country, what do you say when someone compliments you?
What things can you give someone compliments about?

Tapescript

UNIT 1, P. 8

3. Listen and complete the sentences.

1. I have two sons. Do you have <u>children</u>?
2. On weekends, I go shopping. What do you do on <u>weekends</u>?
3. I'm from Mexico. Where are you <u>from</u>?
4. I work in a store. What <u>do you</u> do?
5. Are you single or <u>married</u>?
6. I live downtown. Where do you <u>live</u>?
7. Hi. I'm Susan. What's your <u>name</u>?
8. What do <u>you do</u> on Saturdays and Sundays?

UNIT 1, P. 9

6. Listen to Mr. Sato introduce Susan to other employees at the bicycle factory. Circle the picture of the question Susan asks.

1. Mr. Sato: Tran, this is Susan Gomez. She's our new office manager.
Tran: Hi, Susan. Nice to meet you.
Susan: Nice to meet you too, Tran. Where are you from?
Tran: I'm from Vietnam.
Susan: Oh, that's nice.

2. Mr. Sato: Ivan, this is Susan Gomez. She's our new office manager.
Ivan: Hi, Susan. Nice to meet you.
Susan: Nice to meet you too, Ivan. What do you do here at the bicycle factory?
Ivan: I fix bicycles.
Susan: Oh, that's nice.

3. Mr. Sato: Lisa, this is Susan Gomez. She's our new office manager, and she's also the mother of two children.
Lisa: Hi, Susan. Nice to meet you.
Susan: Nice to meet you too, Lisa. Do you have children?
Lisa: Yes. I have three.
Susan: Oh, that's nice.

4. Mr. Sato: Tom, this is Susan Gomez. She's our new office manager, and I think she lives in your neighborhood.
Tom: Hi, Susan. Nice to meet you.
Susan: Nice to meet you too, Tom. Where do you live?
Tom: I live on 22nd Street.
Susan: Me too!

5. Mr. Sato: Ken? Where are you, Ken?
Ken: Right here, Mr. Sato.
Mr. Sato: What are you doing in there?
Ken: Doing? Uh . . . I'm changing my clothes. . . . I'm getting ready for the weekend.

Mr. Sato: The weekend?!! It's only four o'clock now. You go home at five o'clock!
Ken: Yes, Mr. Sato.
Mr. Sato: Ken, this is Susan Gomez. She's our new office manager.
Ken: Hi, Susan. Nice to meet you.
Susan: Nice to meet you too, Ken. What do you do on weekends?
Ken: I go dancing with my girlfriend, Judy.
Susan: Oh. The secretary?
Ken: Yes.
Susan: That's nice.

Listen again. Complete the answers to Susan's questions.

UNIT 2, P. 12

3. Listen and complete the sentences.

1. I need to clean the floor. Can you give me the <u>mop</u>?
2. I want to dry the dishes. Where's the <u>towel</u>?
3. You can throw that away in the <u>wastebasket</u> over there.
4. I always protect my hands with <u>gloves</u> when I work.
5. I need to cut this paper. Where are the <u>scissors</u>?
6. I want to measure this desk. Can you give me that <u>ruler</u>, please?
7. I need to weigh this letter. Do you have a <u>scale</u>?

UNIT 2, P. 15

7. Ken's coworkers are asking for things. Listen to the conversations. Circle the correct location. If Ken helps, circle *yes*. If Ken can't help, circle *no*.

1. Coworker: Where's the detergent?
Ken: It's in the cabinet.
Coworker: In the cabinet?
Ken: Yes.
Coworker: Can you please bring it to me?
Ken: Sure. No problem.
Coworker: Thanks.

2. Coworker: Where are the gloves?
Ken: They're in the drawer.
Coworker: In the drawer?
Ken: Yes.
Coworker: Can you please bring them to me?
Ken: Sure. No problem.
Coworker: Thanks.

3. Coworker: Where's the pail?
Ken: It's in the closet.
Coworker: In the closet?
Ken: Yes.
Coworker: Can you please bring it to me?
Ken: Sorry, but I'm busy now.
Coworker: OK.

4. Coworker: Where are the scissors?
Ken: They're in the drawer.
Coworker: In the drawer?
Ken: Yes.
Coworker: Can you please bring them to me?
Ken: Sure. No problem.
Coworker: Thanks.

5. Coworker: Hey, it's dark in here. Ken! Where are you?
Ken: Right here! Where are you?
Coworker: Over here. Turn on the light!
Ken: I can't! The lights are out, and I can't see anything!
Coworker: Where are the light bulbs?
Ken: They're in the cabinet.
Coworker: In the cabinet?
Ken: Yes.
Coworker: Can you please bring one to me?
Ken: Sorry, but I can't see the cabinet!
Coworker: I can't see it either!
Ken: Oh, no! What are we going to do?

UNIT 3, P. 19

3. Listen and complete the sentences.

1. The scale is on the second <u>shelf</u>.
2. The sponges are on the middle shelf, on the <u>far left</u>.
3. The mop is <u>behind</u> the wastebasket.
4. The hammer is in the <u>middle of the</u> shelf.
5. The pail is <u>to the left of</u> the iron.
6. The gloves are <u>on top of</u> the towels.
7. The wastebasket is on the <u>bottom</u> shelf.
8. The scissors are <u>below</u> the towels.

UNIT 3, P. 20

6. Listen to six more conversations between Ken and his supervisor. Draw a line from each thing to the correct location in the cabinet.

1. Supervisor: Ken?
Ken: Yes?
Supervisor: Please put this hammer in the cabinet.
Ken: Sure. On which shelf?
Supervisor: On the second shelf, below the screwdriver.
Ken: Second shelf, below the screwdriver. Got it.

2. Supervisor: Ken?
Ken: Yes?
Supervisor: Please put these sponges in the cabinet.
Ken: Sure. On which shelf?
Supervisor: On the middle shelf, on the far left.
Ken: Middle shelf, far left. Got it.

3. Supervisor: Ken?
Ken: Yes?

Supervisor: Please put this scale in the cabinet.
Ken: Sure. On which shelf?
Supervisor: On the bottom shelf, in the middle of the shelf.
Ken: Bottom shelf, in the middle. Got it.

4. Supervisor: Ken?
Ken: Yes?
Supervisor: Please put these pliers in the cabinet.
Ken: Sure. On which shelf?
Supervisor: On the top shelf, to the left of the screwdriver.
Ken: Top shelf, to the left of the screwdriver. Got it.

5. Supervisor: Ken?
Ken: Yes?
Supervisor: Please put this towel in the cabinet.
Ken: Sure. On which shelf?
Supervisor: On the second shelf from the top, above the sponges.
Ken: Second shelf, above the sponges. Got it.

6. Supervisor: Ken?
Ken: Yes?
Supervisor: Please put this detergent in the cabinet.
Ken: Sure. On which shelf?
Supervisor: On the top shelf.
Ken: There's no room on the top shelf.
Supervisor: No room? Then put it on the second shelf.
Ken: There's no room on the second shelf.
Supervisor: Then put it on the second shelf from the bottom.
Ken: There's no room on the second shelf from the bottom.
Supervisor: The bottom shelf, then! Put it on the bottom shelf!
Ken: There's no room on the bottom shelf, either.
Supervisor: So there's no room anywhere in that cabinet?
Ken: There's room on the middle shelf.
Supervisor: Then put the detergent on the middle shelf!

UNIT 4, P. 26

6. Repeat the names of the stores after your teacher. Then listen to the conversations. Circle the correct floor. Then circle *left* or *right*.

1. Judy: Excuse me. I'm looking for a candy shop.
Clerk: Go to the third floor. Sue's Candy Shop is down the hall to the right.
Judy: Third floor, to the right. Thank you.

2. Judy: Excuse me. I'm looking for a toy store.
Clerk: Go to the fifth floor. Toy World is down the hall to the right.
Judy: Fifth floor, to the right. Thank you.

3. Judy: Excuse me. I'm looking for a shoe store.
Clerk: Go to the fourth floor. Guy's Shoe Store is down the hall to the left.
Judy: Fourth floor, to the left. Thank you.

4. Judy: Excuse me. I'm looking for a bakery.
Clerk: Go to the second floor. Eva's Bakery is down the hall to the right.
Judy: Second floor, to the right. Thank you.

5. Judy: Excuse me. I'm looking for a card shop.
Clerk: Go to the fourth floor. Cute Cards is down the hall to the right.
Judy: Fourth floor, to the right. Thank you.

6. Judy: Excuse me. I'm looking for a beauty salon.
Clerk: Go to the fifth floor. Betsy's Beauty Salon is down the hall to the left.
Judy: Fifth floor, to the left. Is it expensive?
Clerk: A haircut is forty dollars.
Judy: Forty dollars? No, thanks! My mother can cut my hair for free!

UNIT 5, P. 30

3. Listen and complete the sentences.

1. Mr. and Mrs. Sato are walking <u>down the street</u>.
2. Tran is going <u>through</u> the window.
3. Lisa and Joe are going <u>across</u> the bridge.
4. Paul and Linda are walking <u>around the block</u>.
5. Carlos is walking <u>to the bottom</u> of the hill.
6. Ruth is walking <u>toward</u> the window.
7. Ken and Judy are going <u>to the top</u> of the hill.
8. Kathy is walking <u>away from</u> the window.

UNIT 5, P. 32

6. Listen to the conversations. Draw a line from the store to the correct location on the map.

1. A: Excuse me. I'm looking for Fine Furniture. Is it near here?
B: Yes, it is. Turn left at the corner.
A: Left at the corner?
B: Yes. Then go across the bridge.
A: Across the bridge?
B: Yes. Then go one block. Fine Furniture is on the corner of Second and Main.
A: Corner of Second and Main. Thank you.

2. A: Excuse me. I'm looking for Toy World. Is it near here?
B: Yes, it is. Go around the corner to the right.
A: Right at the corner?
B: Yes. Then go one block.
A: One block?
B: Yes. Then turn left on Oak. Toy World is in

the middle of the block.
A: Left on Oak. Thank you.

3. A: Excuse me. I'm looking for Low-Cost Drugs. Is it near here?
B: Yes, it is. Turn left at the corner.
A: Left at the corner?
B: Yes. Then turn right on Elm Street.
A: Right on Elm?
B: Yes. Then go along the river three blocks. Low-Cost Drugs is on the corner of Elm and Fifth.
A: Corner of Elm and Fifth. Thank you.

4. A: Excuse me. I'm looking for Betsy's Beauty Salon. Is it near here?
B: Yes, it is. Go around the corner to the right.
A: Right at the corner?
B: Yes. Then turn left on Oak Street.
A: Left on Oak?
B: Yes. Then go up the hill. Betsy's Beauty Salon is at the top of the hill on your right.
A: Top of the hill on the right. Thank you.

5. A: Excuse me. I'm looking for ABC Bookstore. Is it near here?
B: Yes, it is. Turn left at the corner.
A: Left at the corner?
B: Yes. Then go across the bridge.
A: Across the bridge?
B: Yes. Then turn right on River Street. ABC Bookstore is between Third and Fourth Avenue.
A: Right on River. Thank you.

6. A: Excuse me. I'm looking for Dad's Hardware. Is it near here?
B: Yes, it is. Go across the street.
A: Across the street?
B: Yes.
A: Then what?
B: That's it.
A: Dad's Hardware is across the street?
B: Yes. Can't you see it?
A: No. I don't have my glasses. I can't see anything!

UNIT 6, P. 34

3. Listen and complete the sentences.

1. Paul was taking a nap at the <u>day-care center</u>.
2. Mr. and Mrs. Sato were visiting a friend at the <u>hospital</u>.
3. Susan was buying stamps at the <u>post office</u>.
4. Tom and Marsha were looking at pictures at the <u>museum</u>.
5. Ken and Judy were meeting a friend at the <u>bus station</u>.
6. Tran was singing a song in <u>church</u>.
7. Ruth was asking about work at the <u>employment</u> office.
8. Lisa and Joe were talking about a problem at the <u>police station</u>.

UNIT 6, P. 35

4. Listen to the telephone conversations and write the opening and closing times.

1. A: Employment office. Can I help you?
   B: Yes. Can you tell me . . . what are your hours, please?
   A: Well, the office opens at eight o'clock in the morning.
   B: You open at eight. . . .
   A: Uh-huh, and we close at five in the afternoon.
   B: You close at five.
   A: That's right.
   B: Thanks a lot.
   A: You're welcome.

2. A: This is the library. Can I help you?
   B: Yes. Can you tell me . . . what are your hours, please?
   A: Sure. We're open from ten to five thirty.
   B: You said ten to five thirty?
   A: Yup.
   B: Thank you.
   A: Not at all. Bye.

3. A: This is the City Day-Care Center. Can I help you?
   B: Yes. Can you tell me . . . what are your hours, please?
   A: OK. The day-care center opens at seven o'clock in the morning.
   B: Opens at seven. . . .
   A: And we're open until seven o'clock in the evening.
   B: Closes at seven.
   A: That's right.
   B: Got it. Thanks.
   A: You're welcome.

4. A: This is the Art Museum. Can I help you?
   B: Yes. Can you tell me . . . what are your hours, please?
   A: Well, the museum opens at ten in the morning.
   B: Opens at ten. . . .
   A: And we close at half past four.
   B: Closes at half past four. Great. Thanks a lot.
   A: Don't mention it.

5. A: This is the City Clinic. Can I help you?
   B: Yes. Can you tell me . . . what are your hours, please?
   A: Sure. The clinic is open daily from nine thirty to four.
   B: You said nine thirty to four?
   A: That's right.
   B: OK. Thank you.
   A: You're welcome.

6. A: This is the post office. Can I help you?
   B: Yes. Can you tell me . . . what are your hours, please?
   A: Sure can. The post office is open from nine to five.
   B: Nine to what?
   A: Nine to five.
   B: Got it. Thanks.
   A: Not at all.

UNIT 6, P. 38

12. Listen to the conversations. Write the name of the city and the telephone number. Then practice the conversations with a partner.

1. Operator: Operator. What city, please?
   Les: <u>New York.</u>
   Operator: Go ahead.
   Les: Can you tell me the number for the Bank Street Health Clinic?
   Operator: The number is <u>993-2820.</u>

2. Operator: Operator. What city, please?
   Sally: <u>Chicago.</u>
   Operator: Go ahead.
   Sally: Can you tell me the number for the employment office?
   Operator: The number is <u>664-9135.</u>

3. Operator: Operator. What city, please?
   Tony: <u>Dallas.</u>
   Operator: Go ahead.
   Tony: Can you tell me the number for Mercy Hospital?
   Operator: The number is <u>229-7003.</u>

UNIT 7, P. 40

3. Listen and complete the sentences.

1. Can you please tell me where the <u>library</u> is?
2. Excuse me. What time do <u>night classes</u> start at this school?
3. Pardon me. Is there a <u>copy machine</u> at this school?
4. Could you please tell me where the <u>bookstore</u> is?
5. I have a question. Are there any <u>typing</u> classes at this school?
6. Excuse me. Which way is the counselors' <u>office</u>?
7. Pardon me. Are there any <u>computers</u> at this school?
8. Excuse me. How can I get to the <u>listening lab</u>, please?

UNIT 7, P. 44

9. Repeat the names of the classes after your teacher. Then listen to the messages. Write the correct telephone key. Then circle when the classes are and where to go for a registration form.

1. Hello. This is Clay Business College. For information about business classes, press *one*. For information about computer classes, press *two*. For information about typing classes, press *three*.

   At Clay Business College, there are typing classes in the afternoon and at night. To enroll, come to the main office and get a registration form.

2. Hello. This is Ashby Adult School. For information about drivers' education classes, press *one*. For information about ESL classes, press *two*. For information about citizenship classes, press *three*.

   At Ashby Adult School, there are ESL classes in the morning and at night. To enroll, come to the counselors' office and get a registration form.

3. Hello. This is City College. For information about English classes, press *one*. For information about business classes, press *two*. For information about computer classes, press *three*.

At City College, there are computer classes in the morning, in the afternoon, and at night. To enroll, come to the main office and get a registration form.

4. Hello. This is Children's Day School. For information about kindergarten classes, press *one*. For information about swimming classes, press *two*. For information about art classes, press *three*.

At Children's Day School, there are kindergarten classes in the morning only. To enroll your son or daughter, come to the main office and get a registration form.

5. Hello. This is West Community College. For information about ESL classes, press *one*. For information about citizenship classes, press *two*. For information about literacy classes, press *three*.

At West Community College, there are citizenship classes in the morning and at night. To enroll, come to the counselors' office and get a registration form.

6. Hello. This is Ace Auto School. For information about drivers' education classes, press *one*. For information about traffic school, press *two*. For information about auto repair classes, press *three*.

At Ace Auto School, there are drivers' education classes at night only. To enroll, come to the main office and get a registration form.

UNIT 9, P. 53

3. Listen and write the number of each conversation under the correct picture.

1. A: Uh-oh! The gas is leaking!
   B: Oh, no!

2. A: Uh-oh! There are cockroaches on the counter!
   B: Yuck!

3. A: Oh, no, honey. This window is broken.
   B: Don't tell me!

4. A: Darn!
   B: What's wrong?
   A: This faucet is leaking.

5. A: Hmm!
   B: What is it, dear?
   A: The electricity isn't working.

6. A: Look!
   B: Huh?
   A: The ceiling is leaking.

7. A: Oh, no! Problem!
   B: What?
   A: The bathtub's stopped up.

8. A: This milk is bad.

B: You're right. It's not cold.
A: Uh-oh. The refrigerator isn't working.

UNIT 10, P. 60

3. Listen and complete the sentences.

1. Sometimes I <u>return clothes</u> if they're the wrong size.
2. I usually <u>use a credit card</u> when I go shopping.
3. I like to save money, so I sometimes shop at <u>thrift stores</u>.
4. My wife and I <u>worry about</u> money all the time!
5. Sometimes I <u>borrow</u> money at the end of the month.
6. Sometimes my husband and I go to <u>garage sales</u>.
7. I always <u>buy red socks</u> because my girlfriend likes red.
8. I don't like to carry money with me, so I <u>write checks</u> a lot.

UNIT 10, P. 63

9. Does May's Department Store have these things? Listen and check *yes* or *no*. Then circle the correct floor of the store or the shopping center.

1. A: May's Department Store. May I help you?
   B: Yes. Do you sell baby shoes?
   A: Yes, we do. They're on the third floor.
   B: Third floor. Thank you.

2. A: May's Department Store. May I help you?
   B: Yes. Do you sell books?
   A: No, we don't. Try ABC Bookstore. It's on the second floor of the shopping center.
   B: Shopping center, second floor. Thank you.

3. A: May's Department Store. May I help you?
   B: Yes. Do you sell towels?
   A: Yes, we do. They're on the fourth floor.
   B: Fourth floor. Thank you.

4. A: May's Department Store. May I help you?
   B: Yes. Do you sell furniture?
   A: No, we don't. Try Fine Furniture. It's on the third floor of the shopping center.
   B: Shopping center, third floor. Thank you.

5. A: May's Department Store. May I help you?
   B: Yes. Do you sell work gloves?
   A: Yes, we do. They're on the first floor.
   B: First floor. Thank you.

6. A: May's Department Store. May I help you?
   B: Yes. Do you sell mops and pails?
   A: No, we don't.
   B: Oh, no. My bathroom ceiling is leaking. There's water everywhere! What am I going to do?
   A: Try Dad's Hardware. It's on the first floor of the shopping center.
   B: Shopping center, first floor. Thank you!

UNIT 11, P. 66

3. Listen and complete the sentences.

1. Every Friday night, Ken <u>plays cards</u>.
2. On Saturday afternoons, Judy <u>runs in the park</u>.
3. Most Saturdays, Linda and Paul <u>play with their friends</u>.
4. On weeknights, Ken <u>reads books</u> at home.
5. The kids <u>do homework</u> on weeknights.
6. On Saturday, Ken usually <u>plays soccer</u> in the afternoon.
7. On Sundays, Judy doesn't <u>do anything</u>.
8. The kids usually <u>don't do anything</u> on Sundays.

UNIT 11, P. 69

9. Listen to the conversations. Complete the messages.

1. Carlos: Hello?
   Betsy: Hello. May I please speak to Susan?
   Carlos: I'm sorry, but she's not here now. She goes swimming on Sunday afternoons. Would you like to leave a message?
   Betsy: Yes, please. Tell her to call Betsy at Betsy's Beauty Salon. The number is 567-9033.
   Carlos: 567-9033. OK.
   Betsy: Thank you.
   Carlos: You're welcome. Good-bye.

2. Judy: Hello?
   Nurse: Hello. May I please speak to Mr. Sato?
   Judy: I'm sorry, but he's not at work now. He plays golf on Friday afternoons. Would you like to leave a message?
   Nurse: Yes, please. Tell him to call the doctor's office. The number is 864-3509.
   Judy: 864-3509. OK.
   Nurse: Thank you.
   Judy: You're welcome. Good-bye.

3. Susan: Hello?
   Joe: Hello. May I please speak to Carlos?
   Susan: I'm sorry, but he's not here now. He runs in the park on Saturday mornings. Would you like to leave a message?
   Joe: Yes, please. Tell him to call Joe at home. The number is 345-8596.
   Susan: 345-8596. OK.
   Joe: Thank you.
   Susan: You're welcome. Good-bye.

4. Carlos: Hello?
   Kathy: Hello. May I please speak to Linda?
   Carlos: I'm sorry, but she's not here now. She goes to a friend's house on Saturdays. Would you like to leave a message?
   Kathy: Yes, please. Tell her to call Kathy at home. The number is 664-9046.
   Carlos: 664-9046. OK.
   Kathy: Thank you.
   Carlos: You're welcome. Good-bye.

5. Susan: Hello?
   Dad: Hello. May I please speak to Carlos?
   Susan: I'm sorry, but Carlos isn't here now. He plays cards on Saturday afternoons. Would you like to leave a message?
   Dad: Yes, please. Tell him to call Dad at Dad's Hardware. The number is 689-7990.
   Susan: 689-7990. OK.
   Dad: Thank you.
   Susan: You're welcome. Good-bye.

6. Mrs. Wong: Hello?
   Judy: Hi, Mrs. Wong. It's Judy. May I please speak to Ken?
   Mrs. Wong: I'm sorry, Judy, but Ken's not here now.
   Judy: He isn't? Where is he?
   Mrs. Wong: He's at a movie.
   Judy: A movie? Who's he with?
   Mrs. Wong: Well, uh, I think he might be with Eva.
   Judy: Eva?!! He's at a movie with Eva?!!
   Mrs. Wong: Would you like to leave a message, Judy?
   Judy: Yes, please! Tell him to call me right away at 667-3452. He probably doesn't have my number anymore!
   Mrs. Wong: 667-3452. OK.
   Judy: Thanks a lot!
   Mrs. Wong: You're welcome. Good-bye.

UNIT 12, P. 73

3. Listen and write the number of each conversation under the correct picture

1. Interviewer: What kind of work do you do?
   Peter: I'm an electrician.
   Interviewer: I see, an electrician. And your name?
   Peter: Peter.
   Interviewer: Peter?
   Peter: Right. P-e-t-e-r.

2. Interviewer: Your occupation, please?
   Lisa: I'm a fire fighter.
   Interviewer: Mm-hmm, a fire fighter. And your name?
   Lisa: Lisa.
   Interviewer: Pardon me?
   Lisa: Lisa. L-i-s-a.

3. Interviewer: What's your job, please?
   Sally: I'm a dentist.
   Interviewer: A dentist, huh? And your name?
   Sally: Sally.
   Interviewer: How do you spell that?
   Sally: S-a-l-l-y. Sally.

4. Interviewer: What's your occupation, please?
   Andy: I'm a plumber.
   Interviewer: I see, a plumber. And your name?
   Andy: Andy.
   Interviewer: Excuse me?
   Andy: Andy. A-n-d-y.

5. Interviewer: What do you do?
Joe: I'm a mechanic.
Interviewer: A mechanic, is it? And your name?
Joe: Joe.
Interviewer: Joe?
Joe: That's right. J-o-e.

6. Interviewer: What kind of work do you do?
Marsha: I'm a seamstress.
Interviewer: Oh, a seamstress. And your name, please?
Marsha: Marsha.
Interviewer: How do you spell that?
Marsha: M-a-r-s-h-a. Marsha.

7. Interviewer: What's your job, please?
Ruth: I'm a mail carrier.
Interviewer: Oh, a mail carrier. And your name?
Ruth: Ruth.
Interviewer: That was Ruth?
Ruth: Uh-huh. R-u-t-h.

8. Interviewer: What's your occupation, please?
Ivan: I'm a janitor.
Interviewer: A janitor, huh? And your name is . . . ?
Ivan: Ivan.
Interviewer: You said Ivan?
Ivan: That's right. I-v-a-n.

9. Interviewer: What kind of work do you do?
Marco: I'm a police officer.
Interviewer: A police officer! Gee. And your name, sir?
Marco: Marco.
Interviewer: Really? That's my name too! You mean M-a-r-c-o?
Marco: That's right. Nice to meet you, Marco.
Interviewer: Nice to meet you, Marco!

UNIT 12, P. 73

4. Listen and complete the sentences.

1. My name's Joe, and I repair cars. I'm a <u>mechanic</u>.
2. I'm Marsha, and I sew clothes. I'm a <u>seamstress</u>.
3. My name is Carlos, and I work on houses. I'm a <u>construction worker</u>.
4. I'm Ken. I work as a <u>stock clerk</u> at the bicycle company.
5. My name is Sally. I take care of people's teeth. I'm a <u>dentist</u>.
6. I'm Andy, and I fix the pipes in people's homes. I'm a <u>plumber</u>.
7. My name is Ivan, and I work cleaning offices. I'm a <u>janitor</u>.
8. I'm Kathy, and I'm a <u>waitress</u> in a restaurant.

UNIT 12, P. 76

9. Read the Help Wanted ads with your teacher. Then listen to the people talk about their job qualifications. Circle *yes* if the person can do the job. Circle *no* if the person can't do the job.

1. Hello. My name is Andy Smith. I'm a plumber, and I'm looking for a new job. I have a car, and, of course, I have a driver's license too. I also have my own plumbing tools. I can start work anytime. I have six years' experience.

2. Hello. My name is Kathy Lane. I'm a seamstress, and I'm looking for a new job. I can sew everything—dresses, shirts, blouses, and pants. I have eight years' experience. I can work anytime—in the morning, in the afternoon, or at night. I want a full-time job.

3. Hello. My name is Debbie Lopez. I'm a secretary, and I'm looking for a new job. I have four years' experience as a secretary. I type fifty-five words a minute, and I have experience working on computers. I speak two languages—English and Spanish.

4. Hello. My name is Tony Snyder. I'm a college student, and I'm looking for a job. I take classes in the morning, but I can work in the afternoon and on weekends. I'd like to try construction work. I don't have any experience as a construction worker, but I'm good with tools. I can drive, but I don't have my own truck.

5. Ken: Hello. My name is Ken Wong. I'm a stock clerk at the Ace Bicycle Factory. At work, I lift a lot of heavy things. I like my job OK, but the pay is too low. So I'm looking for a new job and more money.
Mr. Sato: Ken?
Ken: Yes, Mr. Sato?
Mr. Sato: What are you doing?
Ken: Oh, nothing.
Mr. Sato: Are you reading the newspaper?
Ken: No! Mr. Sato—uh, er, yes. I was . . . looking at the front page. . . .
Mr. Sato: You were looking at the Help Wanted ads!
Ken: The Help Wanted ads? Well, sir, I . . .
Mr. Sato: Put them away! I know you need more money, so I'm raising your salary to $7.50 an hour. Now throw that newspaper away and get to work!
Ken: OK, boss! I guess I don't need that new job after all.

UNIT 13, P. 78

3. Listen and complete the sentences.

1. All the people in my office can <u>type</u>.
2. My sister likes to sew, and she can <u>alter clothes</u>.
3. I use machines, but I can't <u>repair machines</u>.
4. Be careful when you use <u>electric tools</u>!
5. When you travel, it's important to <u>read maps</u>.
6. I like to make things, so I often use <u>hand tools</u>.
7. These days, most people can use a <u>calculator</u>.
8. I can only drive a car, but my sister can <u>drive a truck.</u>

UNIT 13, P. 81

9. Listen to people calling for job interviews. Circle the correct job. Then write the day and time of the interview and the address.

1. **Joe:** Joe's Auto Works. Joe speaking.
   Tony: Hello. My name is Tony Lopez. I'm calling about the job as a mechanic. I have six years' experience.
   Joe: I see. Can you come in for an interview?
   Tony: Yes, I can. When?
   Joe: How about Wednesday morning at ten o'clock?
   Tony: Wednesday at ten is fine. What's the address?
   Joe: 1227 Brewer Street.
   Tony: 1227 Brewer? Can you spell that, please?
   Joe: Sure. It's B-r-e-w-e-r.
   Tony: B-r-e-w-e-r. OK, Joe. I'll be there at ten on Wednesday.

2. **Receptionist:** Pacific Travel.
   Marsha: Hello. May I please speak to Mrs. Lo?
   Receptionist: Just a minute, please.
   Mrs. Lo: This is Mrs. Lo.
   Marsha: Hello. My name is Marsha Wong. I'm calling about the job as a secretary. I speak English and Chinese.
   Mrs. Lo: I see. Can you come in for an interview?
   Marsha: Yes, I can. When?
   Mrs. Lo: How about Friday afternoon at four thirty?
   Marsha: Friday at four thirty is fine. What's the address?
   Mrs. Lo: 764 Gough Street.
   Marsha: 764 Gough? Can you spell that, please?
   Mrs. Lo: Sure. It's G-o-u-g-h.
   Marsha: G-o-u-g-h. OK, Mrs. Lo. I'll be there at four thirty on Friday.

3. **May:** May's Cafeteria. May speaking.
   Lisa: Hello. My name is Lisa Adams. I'm calling about the job as a cashier. I have nine months' experience.
   May: I see. Can you come in for an interview?
   Lisa: Yes, I can. When?
   May: How about tomorrow morning at nine o'clock?
   Lisa: Tomorrow at nine is fine. What's the address?
   May: 2205 Jayne Street.
   Lisa: 2205 Jayne? Can you spell that, please?
   May: Sure. It's J-a-y-n-e.
   Lisa: J-a-y-n-e. OK, May. I'll be there at nine tomorrow.

4. **Mr. Tong:** Eastside Bank. Mr. Tong speaking.
   Tom: Hello. My name is Tom Baker. I'm calling about the job as a security guard. I can work the night shift.
   Mr. Tong: I see. Can you come in for an interview?
   Tom: Yes, I can. When?

Mr. Tong: How about Thursday evening at seven o'clock?
Tom: Thursday at seven is fine. What's the address?
Mr. Tong: 92 Boren Avenue.
Tom: 92 Boren? Can you spell that, please?
Mr. Tong: Sure. It's B-o-r-e-n.
Tom: B-o-r-e-n. Hey, is Boren between Jackson and Broadway?
Mr. Tong: Yes. Why?
Tom: That's *my* neighborhood! I live on Jackson just two blocks down the street! Wow! Now I really want this job!
Mr. Tong: OK, but first you have to come for the interview . . .
Tom: Wow! I can walk to work!
Mr. Tong: Well, maybe . . .
Tom: No more buses!
Mr. Tong: Let's wait and see . . .
Tom: OK, Mr. Tong! I'll be there at seven on Thursday. Thanks!

UNIT 14, P. 88

9. For each question, read the answers first with your teacher. Then listen to the question and circle the letter of the correct answer.

1. Can you speak Spanish?
2. Where do you work now?
3. Are you looking for a full-time job?
4. When can you start work?
5. Do you have experience as an electrician?
6. How much experience do you have?
7. Can you work the night shift?
8. Do you have experience with computers?
9. Are you looking for a part-time job?
10. Do you have a driver's license?

UNIT 15, P. 93

3. Listen and complete the sentences.

1. Bring some warm clothes for Linda. She has a <u>fever</u>.
2. Quick! Help Mrs. Sato sit down. She feels <u>dizzy</u>.
3. Mr. Sato eats too much candy, and now he has a <u>toothache</u>.
4. Andy doesn't want to do anything. He feels <u>run-down</u>.
5. Paul talked all night last night, and now he has a <u>sore throat</u>.
6. Lisa is holding her stomach because she has <u>cramps</u>.
7. Judy ate some bad food, and now she feels <u>sick to her stomach</u>.
8. Marsha's arm is all red. She has a <u>rash</u>.

8. Judy's coworkers aren't feeling well. Listen to the conversations and put a check above the correct health problem.

1. **Judy:** Hi, Susan. How are you?
   Susan: Hi, Judy. I'm not feeling very well.
   Judy: What's the matter?
   Susan: I have a toothache.
   Judy: Why don't you see a dentist? Maybe you have a cavity.
   Susan: A cavity? Hmm. Maybe you're right. Thanks for the advice.

2. **Judy:** Hi, Ivan. How are you?
   Ivan: Hi, Judy. I'm not feeling very well.
   Judy: What's the matter?
   Ivan: I feel run-down.
   Judy: Why don't you see a doctor? Maybe you need a shot.
   Ivan: A shot? Hmm. Maybe you're right. Thanks for the advice.

3. **Judy:** Hi, Mr. Sato. How are you?
   Mr. Sato: Hi, Judy. I'm not feeling very well.
   Judy: What's the matter?
   Mr. Sato: I have the chills.
   Judy: Why don't you take your temperature with this thermometer? Maybe you have a fever.
   Mr. Sato: A fever? Hmm. Maybe you're right. Thanks for the advice.

4. **Judy:** Hi, Ruth. How are you?
   Ruth: Hi, Judy. I'm not feeling very well.
   Judy: What's the matter?
   Ruth: My ear hurts.
   Judy: Why don't you see a doctor? Maybe you have an infection.
   Ruth: An infection? Hmm. Maybe you're right. Thanks for the advice.

5. **Judy:** Hi, Ken. How are you?
   Ken: Hi, Judy. I'm not feeling very well.
   Judy: What's the matter?
   Ken: I feel sick to my stomach.
   Judy: Why don't you go home? Maybe you need some rest.
   Ken: Some rest? I don't know. Oh, no! I think I need a bathroom. I need a bathroom right now!

   Now listen again. Complete Judy's advice.

UNIT 15, P. 96

9. Listen to the conversation and write the missing words. Then practice the conversation with a partner.

Judy: Hi, Carlos. How are you?
Carlos: Hi, Judy. I'm not feeling very well.
Judy: What's the <u>matter</u>?
Carlos: I feel hot and <u>dizzy</u>.

Judy: Why don't you take your <u>temperature</u> with this thermometer? Maybe you have a <u>fever</u>.
Carlos: A fever? Hmm. Maybe you're right. Thanks for the <u>advice</u>.

UNIT 16, P. 100

3. Listen and complete the sentences.

1. Next Wednesday, Ken and Judy are going to <u>go skiing</u>.
2. Susan is going to <u>stay home</u> next Wednesday.
3. Carlos is going to <u>have an operation</u> next Wednesday.
4. Next Tuesday, the cat is going to <u>drink soda</u>.
5. Carlos is going to <u>check into the hospital</u> next Tuesday.
6. Susan is going to <u>have a tooth pulled</u> next Tuesday.
7. Are Ken and Judy going to <u>feel bad</u> on Thursday?
8. Is Susan going to <u>eat ice cream</u> on Thursday?

UNIT 16, P. 104

9. Listen to other Ace Bicycle Factory employees call in sick to work. Write their health problems. Then circle *yes*, *no*, or *not sure*.

1. **Judy:** Ace Bicycle Factory. Judy speaking.
   Ivan: Hello, Judy. This is Ivan Sims. I'm not going to come to work today. I'm sick.
   Judy: Oh, no. What's the matter?
   Ivan: My throat hurts. I think I have a throat infection.
   Judy: I'm sorry to hear that. Are you going to come in tomorrow?
   Ivan: No, I don't think so.
   Judy: OK. I hope you feel better soon.
   Ivan: Thanks. Good-bye.

2. **Judy:** Ace Bicycle Factory. Judy speaking.
   Ruth: Hello, Judy. This is Ruth Laman. I'm not going to come to work today. I'm sick.
   Judy: Oh, no. What's the matter?
   Ruth: I have cramps.
   Judy: I'm sorry to hear that. Are you going to come in tomorrow?
   Ruth: Yes, I am.
   Judy: OK. I hope you feel better soon.
   Ruth: Thanks. Good-bye.

3. **Judy:** Ace Bicycle Factory. Judy speaking.
   Mr. Sato: Hello, Judy. This is Mr. Sato. I'm not going to come to work today.
   Judy: Oh, no. What's the matter?
   Mr. Sato: My tooth hurts. I think I have a cavity, so I'm going to the dentist.
   Judy: I'm sorry to hear that. Are you going to come in tomorrow?
   Mr. Sato: Yes, I am.
   Judy: OK. I hope you feel better soon.
   Mr. Sato: Thanks. Good-bye.

4. **Judy:** Ace Bicycle Factory. Judy speaking.
   Tran: Hello, Judy. This is Tran Ng. I'm not going to come to work today. I'm sick.

Judy: Oh, no. What's the matter?

Tran: My ear hurts. I think I have an ear infection.

Judy: I'm sorry to hear that. Are you going to come in tomorrow?

Tran: I'm not sure.

Judy: OK. I hope you feel better soon.

Tran: Thanks. Good-bye.

5. **Judy:** Ace Bicycle Factory. Judy speaking.

Marco: Hello, J-J-Judy. This is M-M-Marco Garcia. I'm n-n-not going to come to work today. I'm s-s-sick.

Judy: Oh, no, Marco. You sound terrible. What's the matter?

Marco: I have the ch-ch-ch . . . I have the ch-ch-chills.

Judy: I'm sorry to hear that. Are you going to come in tomorrow?

Marco: M-M-Maybe. If I can find some w-w-warm clothes.

Judy: Warm clothes? Marco, you don't need warm clothes. You need to get in bed and stay there!

Marco: OK, Judy. Thanks. G-G-Good-bye.

UNIT 17, P. 109

6. Listen to other people ordering services. Check the correct service and write the date of the move.

1. **Receptionist:** Bayside Garbage Collection. May I help you?

Ruth: Yes. I'd like service for my new apartment.

Receptionist: Do you have an account with our garbage service now?

Ruth: No, I don't.

Receptionist: What's your name?

Ruth: Ruth Laman.

Receptionist: What's the address?

Ruth: 272 Main Street, Apartment 7.

Receptionist: When are you going to move?

Ruth: March 15th.

Receptionist: All right, Ms. Laman. There's a deposit of $25.

Ruth: $25. Thank you. Good-bye.

2. **Receptionist:** Owens Electric Company. May I help you?

Ivan: Yes. I'd like service for my new house.

Receptionist: Do you have an account with the electric company now?

Ivan: Yes, I do.

Receptionist: What's your name?

Ivan: Ivan Sims.

Receptionist: What's the new address?

Ivan: 839 Union Street.

Receptionist: When are you going to move?

Ivan: January 1st.

Receptionist: All right, Mr. Sims.

Ivan: Is there a deposit?

Receptionist: No, there isn't.

Ivan: Thank you. Good-bye.

3. **Receptionist:** Statewide Telephone Company. May I help you?

Marco: Yes. I'd like service for my new apartment.

Receptionist: Do you have an account with the phone company now?

Marco: No, I don't.

Receptionist: What's your name?

Marco: Marco Garcia.

Receptionist: What's the address?

Marco: 79 Hill Street, Apartment 1.

Receptionist: When are you going to move?

Marco: August 15th.

Receptionist: All right, Mr. Garcia. Your new phone number is 789-2127.

Marco: 789-2127.

Receptionist: That's right. And there's a deposit of $45.

Marco: $45. Thank you. Good-bye.

4. **Receptionist:** Westside Gas Company. May I help you?

Tran: Yes. I'd like service for my new apartment.

Receptionist: Do you have an account with the gas company now?

Tran: Yes, I do.

Receptionist: What's your name?

Tran: Tran Ng.

Receptionist: What's the new address?

Tran: 1115 Geary Street, Apartment 42.

Receptionist: When are you going to move?

Tran: October 25th.

Receptionist: All right, Mr. Ng.

Tran: Is there a deposit?

Receptionist: No, there isn't.

Tran: Thank you. Good-bye.

5. **Receptionist:** Gray's Garbage Collection. May I help you?

Mr. Sato: Yes. I'd like service for my new store.

Receptionist: Do you have an account with our garbage service now?

Mr. Sato: No, I don't.

Receptionist: What's your name?

Mr. Sato: Gary Sato.

Receptionist: What's the address?

Mr. Sato: 1205 Main Street.

Receptionist: When is your new store going to open?

Mr. Sato: May 1st.

Receptionist: All right, Mr. Sato. There's a deposit of $400.

Mr. Sato: $400?!!

Receptionist: Yes. There's a $400 deposit for new accounts with stores.

Mr. Sato: I'm sorry, but $400 is too much money!

Receptionist: Then you don't want an account with us?

Mr. Sato: No, thank you! I'll empty the garbage myself!

Listen again. Is there a deposit? Circle *yes* or *no*. If you circle *yes*, write the amount.

UNIT 18, P. 112

3. Listen and complete the sentences.

1. Sometimes I feel lonely here. Will I go back to <u>my country</u> someday?

2. When I get old, will I have <u>white hair</u>?

3. My pay is so low! When will I <u>get a raise</u>?

4. I want to see many places. Will I <u>travel around</u> the world someday?

5. I always work hard. When will I get a <u>promotion</u>?

6. I don't like to be poor! Will I <u>be rich</u> in the future?

7. My work isn't very interesting. When will I get a <u>new job</u>?

8. I always see the president on TV. <u>Will I meet</u> him in my lifetime?

UNIT 18, P. 115

9. Listen to Susan's conversations with friends and family. Put a check above the thing each person wants to borrow. Then write when the person will return it.

1. Tony: Hi, Susan.
   Susan: Hi, Tony. How are you?
   Tony: I'm fine, thanks. Susan, can you do me a favor?
   Susan: What is it?
   Tony: Can I borrow that pail over there? I have to water my garden.
   Susan: That pail? Sure. Take it for as long as you like.
   Tony: Thanks. I'll return it tomorrow. See you then.
   Susan: Good-bye.

2. Peter: Hi, Susan.
   Susan: Hi, Peter. How are you?
   Peter: I'm fine, thanks. Susan, can you do me a favor?
   Susan: What is it?
   Peter: Can I borrow your broom? I have to sweep the floor.
   Susan: My broom? Sure. I'll get it for you right now. Here you go.
   Peter: Thanks. I'll return it in two hours. See you later.
   Susan: Good-bye.

3. Debbie: Hi, Susan.
   Susan: Hi, Debbie. How are you?
   Debbie: I'm fine, thanks. Susan, can you do me a favor?
   Susan: What is it?
   Debbie: Do you have a hammer?
   Susan: A hammer? Yes. Why?
   Debbie: Can I borrow it? I have to fix my sofa.
   Susan: Sure. I'll get it for you right now. Here you go.
   Debbie: Thanks. I'll return it this evening. See you later.
   Susan: Good-bye.

4. Les: Hi, Susan.
   Susan: Hi, Les. How are you?
   Les: I'm fine, thanks. Susan, can you do me a favor?
   Susan: What is it?
   Les: Do you have a screwdriver?
   Susan: A screwdriver? Yes. Why?
   Les: Can I borrow it? I have to fix my bicycle.
   Susan: Sure. I'll get it for you right now. Here you go.
   Les: Thanks. I'll return it in a few minutes. See you soon.
   Susan: Good-bye.

5. Eva: Hi, Susan.
   Susan: Hi, Eva. How are you?
   Eva: I'm fine, thanks. Susan, can you do me a favor?
   Susan: What is it?
   Eva: Can I borrow your thermometer? I have to take Kathy's temperature.
   Susan: My thermometer? Sure. I'll get it for you right now. Here you go.
   Eva: Thanks. I'll return it tomorrow night. See you then.
   Susan: Good-bye.

6. Betsy: Hi, Susan.
   Susan: Hi, Betsy. How are you?
   Betsy: I'm fine, thanks. Susan, can you do me a favor?
   Susan: What is it?
   Betsy: Can I borrow your sewing scissors? I have to cut out a dress.
   Susan: My scissors? Sure. I'll get them for you right now. Here you go.
   Betsy: Thanks. I'll return them tonight. See you later.
   Susan: Good-bye.

7. Sam: Hi, Susan.
   Susan: Hi, Sam. How are you?
   Sam: I'm fine, thanks. Susan, can you do me a favor?
   Susan: What is it?
   Sam: Do you have a small scale?
   Susan: A small scale? Yes. Why?
   Sam: Can I borrow it? I have to weigh some letters.
   Susan: Sure. I'll get it for you right now. Here you go.
   Sam: Thanks. I'll return it at dinnertime. See you later.
   Susan: Good-bye.

8. **Carlos:** Hi, Susan.
   Susan: Hi, Carlos. How you doing?
   Carlos: OK. Honey, can I borrow a dollar?
   Susan: A dollar? Sure. What for?
   Carlos: Oh, I'm a little hungry. I have to eat something.
   Susan: Why don't you eat some of that salad in the refrigerator?
   Carlos: Salad? Nah . . . I don't want salad.
   Susan: How about some of that carrot soup?
   Carlos: Huh-uh. I don't want carrot soup. I want candy!
   Susan: Candy? Oh, Carlos. Why don't you eat healthy food?
   Carlos: I do. But candy is good too!
   Susan: Oh, all right! Here's a dollar.
   Carlos: Thanks. I'll return it tomorrow.
   Susan: I can't wait.

UNIT 19, P. 118

3. Listen and complete the questions.

1. When did Ken and Judy <u>borrow money</u>?
2. What day did Carlos <u>open a bank</u> account?
3. Why did the cat <u>chase mice</u> on Tuesday?
4. Where did Ken and Judy <u>gamble all day</u>?
5. Why did Carlos close the <u>bank account</u>?
6. What day did Ken and Judy <u>return the money</u>?
7. Where did Carlos <u>shop all day</u>?
8. When did Carlos <u>deposit money</u> in his account?

UNIT 19, P. 121

9. Listen to questions about the conversations above. Circle the letter of the correct answer.

1. What kind of account did Carlos open?
2. How much money did Carlos deposit?
3. What is the service charge on Carlos's account?
4. What kind of account did Judy open?
5. How much money did Judy deposit?
6. What is the interest on Judy's account?

UNIT 19, P. 122

10. Listen to the teller talk about checking and savings accounts. Then read about them. Ask your teacher if you don't understand.

We have two kinds of checking accounts here at Bayside Bank.

The first is our Regular Checking Account. There's no minimum balance required—you can keep any amount of money in the account. For our Regular Checking Account, there's a service charge of $7 a month.

The second is our Super Checking Account. There's a minimum balance of $1,000 required—you must keep $1,000 in the account. But for our Super Checking

Account, there's no service charge. It doesn't cost anything to keep your money in this account.

We have two kinds of savings accounts here at Bayside Bank.

The first is our Regular Savings Account. There's no minimum balance required—you can keep any amount of money in the account. The interest on our Regular Savings Account is 4%.

The second is our Super Savings Account. There's a minimum balance of $2,000 required—you must keep $2,000 in the account. But you earn more interest with our Super Savings Account. The interest on the account is 5%.

UNIT 20, P. 124

3. Listen and complete the sentences.

1. On weekends, my family often <u>watches movies</u>.
2. In high school, I <u>played sports</u> with my classmates.
3. My husband and I love music, so we often <u>attended concerts</u>.
4. Many people <u>studied English</u> in school in my country.
5. My wife and I sometimes <u>shopped at</u> department stores.
6. I like art, so I often <u>visited museums</u> on the weekends.
7. When my friends and I traveled, we usually <u>used trains</u>.
8. I love to read, so I often <u>used the library</u> near my house.

UNIT 20, P. 126

8. Listen to Carlos. Then listen to the questions and circle the letter of the correct answer.

Carlos: Hey, Susan. This postal notice was on our front door today.
Susan: Oh. What did we get? A letter?
Carlos: No. A parcel.
Susan: A parcel. Hmm. Who's it from?
Carlos: It's from my brother Marco.
Susan: Oh. Well, we're not going to be home when the mail comes tomorrow. Can we pick it up at the post office?
Carlos: Yes. We can pick it up at the post office after 10:00 A.M. I'll stop by on my lunch break tomorrow.
Susan: OK. What is it, I wonder?
Carlos: Maybe it's a box of candy!
Susan: Candy?! I hope not. You're getting too fat!

1. Did the mail carrier leave a parcel for Carlos?
2. Did the mail carrier leave the notice on the front door?
3. Did Susan find the notice?

4. Did Carlos's mother send the parcel?

5. Did Marco send the parcel?

6. Did Carlos ask Susan to pick up the parcel?

UNIT 20, P. 127

10. Listen to other conversations at the post office. Check the correct kind of mail. If the customers pick up their mail, circle *yes*. If they don't pick it up, circle *no* and write when they can come back.

1. **Clerk:** Next, please.
   Woman: Hello. This notice was on my front door yesterday.
   Clerk: Let's see. Yes. We have a magazine for you. I'll go get it. And I'll need to see a picture ID. . . . I'm sorry, ma'am. The magazine isn't here yet.
   Woman: When can I pick it up?
   Clerk: Come back tomorrow morning.
   Woman: Thank you.

2. **Clerk:** Next, please.
   Man: Hello. This notice was on my front door yesterday.
   Clerk: Let's see. Yes. We have a package for you with something perishable. I'll go get it. And I'll need to see a picture ID. . . . Here it is, sir.
   Man: Here's my driver's license.
   Clerk: That's fine.
   Man: Thank you.

3. **Clerk:** Next, please.
   Man: Hello. This notice was on my front door yesterday.
   Clerk: Let's see. Yes. We have a letter that you need to sign. I'll go get it. And I'll need to see a picture ID. . . . Here it is, sir.
   Man: Here's my driver's license.
   Clerk: That's fine.
   Man: Thank you.

4. **Clerk:** Next, please.
   Woman: Hello. This notice was on my front door yesterday.
   Clerk: Let's see. Yes. We have a large envelope for you. I'll go get it. And I'll need to see a picture ID. . . . I'm sorry, ma'am. The envelope isn't here yet.
   Woman: When can I pick it up?
   Clerk: Come back tomorrow afternoon.
   Woman: Thank you.

5. **Clerk:** Next, please.
   Carlos: Hello. This notice was on my front door two days ago.
   Clerk: Let's see. Yes. We have a parcel for you. I'll go get it. And I'll need to see a picture ID.
   Carlos: Here's my driver's license. Carlos Gomez.
   Clerk: Here it is, Mr. Gomez. It's pretty heavy.
   Carlos: Oh, no.

Clerk: Don't worry, sir. I can carry it out to the car for you.
Carlos: It's not that. I wanted candy!!
Clerk: Candy? Well, this sure isn't candy!
Carlos: Oh, well. Thanks anyway.

UNIT 21, P. 133

8. Listen to other conversations at the department store. Circle the problem with the clothing. Then check *return* or *exchange* and write what the customer gets.

1. **Salesclerk:** Hello. May I help you?
   Customer: Yes. I bought this coat for my mother, but it's too big.
   Salesclerk: What size is it?
   Customer: It's size fourteen.
   Salesclerk: Do you want to return it or exchange it for a size twelve?
   Customer: I'd like to exchange it, please. Here's the receipt.
   Salesclerk: And here's the coat in size twelve.
   Customer: Thank you.

2. **Salesclerk:** Hello. May I help you?
   Customer: Yes. I bought these pants for my son, but they're too small.
   Salesclerk: What size are they?
   Customer: They're size thirty.
   Salesclerk: Do you want to return them or exchange them for size thirty-two?
   Customer: I'd like to exchange them, please. Here's the receipt.
   Salesclerk: And here are the pants in size thirty-two.
   Customer: Thank you.

3. **Salesclerk:** Hello. May I help you?
   Customer: Yes. I bought these shorts for my sister, but they're too big.
   Salesclerk: What size are they?
   Customer: They're medium.
   Salesclerk: Do you want to return them or exchange them for a small?
   Customer: I'd like to return them, please. Here's the receipt.
   Salesclerk: And here's your money—$12.95.
   Customer: Thank you.

4. **Salesclerk:** Hello. May I help you?
   Customer: Yes. I bought this belt for my husband, but it's too small.
   Salesclerk: What size is it?
   Customer: It's size thirty-two.
   Salesclerk: Do you want to return it or exchange it for a size thirty-four?
   Customer: I'd like to return it, please. Here's the receipt.
   Salesclerk: And here's your money—$40.29.
   Customer: Thank you.

5. Salesclerk: Hello. May I help you?
   Customer: Yes. I bought this blouse for my girlfriend, but it's too small.
   Salesclerk: What size is it?
   Customer: It's a size seven.
   Salesclerk: Do you want to return it or exchange it for a size nine?
   Customer: I'd like to return it, please. Here's the receipt.
   Salesclerk: Oh, I'm sorry. This blouse was on sale. You can't return it, but you can exchange it.
   Customer: Oh, no. My girlfriend hates this blouse!
   Salesclerk: Well, why don't you look for something different? A skirt, maybe?
   Customer: I don't know. My girlfriend says I don't know how to buy nice clothes.
   Salesclerk: Well, maybe I can help you.
   Customer: Help me? Would you really help me?
   Salesclerk: Of course. That's my job.
   Customer: Oh, thank you. Thank you so much!
   Salesclerk: Now how about this blue skirt?

UNIT 21, P. 134

9. Listen to the conversation and write the missing words. Then practice it with a partner.

   Salesclerk: Hello. May I help you?
   Customer: Yes. I bought this <u>dress</u> for my <u>wife</u>, but it's too <u>big</u>.
   Salesclerk: What size is it?
   Customer: It's size <u>ten</u>.
   Salesclerk: Do you want to return it or exchange it for a size <u>eight</u>?
   Customer: I'd like to return it, please. Here's the receipt.
   Salesclerk: Oh, I'm sorry. This <u>dress</u> was on sale. You can't return it, but you can <u>exchange</u> it for something else.
   Customer: I see. Then maybe I'll look for a <u>jacket</u>.

UNIT 22, P. 137

3. Listen and complete the sentences.

1. Quick! Get a bandage. Susan <u>fell down</u> and cut her head!
2. Oh, no! Poor Linda got an <u>electric</u> shock!
3. Please help! Mr. Sato can't breathe. <u>He's choking</u>.
4. Call 911! Joe was crossing the street and a <u>car hit</u> him.
5. Hurry! Get some ice. Carlos <u>burned</u> his hand.
6. Quick! Stop Paul! He's drinking <u>poison</u>.
7. Get a bandage. Judy's hand <u>is bleeding</u>.
8. Mrs. Sato is having <u>chest pains</u>. Call the doctor.
9. Get water to wash Ken's foot. He <u>stepped</u> on a nail.
10. Quick! Call 911. Susan is on the floor. She <u>passed out.</u>

UNIT 22, P. 138

4. Listen and write the number of each conversation under the correct picture.

1. A: Oh, no!
   B: What?
   A: It's Judy. A dog bit her. Her hand is bleeding.
   B: Let's get a bandage.

2. A: Quick! Help! Joe was hit by a car!
   B: Joe?
   A: Yes. He's unconscious.
   B: Let's call 911.

3. A: Uh-oh! Carlos burned himself.
   B: Huh?
   A: Carlos was ironing a shirt, and he burned himself.
   B: Let's get some ice, quick.

4. A: Oh, my goodness!
   B: What?
   A: It's Paul! He drank poison.
   B: Oh, no! Is he unconscious?

5. A: Help! Please!
   B: What's wrong?
   A: Mrs. Sato is having chest pains.
   B: Tell her to sit down. I'll call the doctor.

6. A: Oh, no!
   B: What is it?
   A: It's Susan. She fell down.
   B: Is she bleeding?
   A: Yes.
   B: Let's take her to the emergency room.

7. A: Linda!! Linda, no!
   B: What is it, dear?
   A: It's Linda. She got an electric shock.
   B: Oh, no! Let's call 911.

8. A: Help!
   B: What's the matter?
   A: It's Mr. Sato. He's choking!
   B: Is he coughing?
   A: Yes.
   B: Well, let him cough.

9. A: What happened to Ken?
   B: He stepped on a nail.
   A: What?
   B: Yeah. Let's take him to the doctor.

Now listen again and write each person's name beside the number.

UNIT 22, P. 139

7. Listen to the conversations and write the number of each conversation under the correct picture. Then write what's coming: an ambulance, a fire truck, or a police car.

1. Operator: 911 Emergency.
   Ken: Hello. I'm calling to report a car accident. The drivers are unconscious.

Operator: What's your name?
Ken: Ken Wong.
Operator: What's your address?
Ken: 3506 Baker Street.
Operator: And where is the accident?
Ken: At the corner of Baker and Thirty-fifth.
Operator: OK. We'll send an ambulance right away.
Ken: Thank you. Good-bye.

2. Operator: 911 Emergency.
Judy: Hello. I need help. A person I don't know is trying to get inside my neighbor's house.
Operator: What's your name?
Judy: Judy Johnson.
Operator: What's your address?
Judy: 762 Vine Street.
Operator: What's your neighbor's address?
Judy: 766 Vine Street.
Operator: OK. Stay inside your house, Ms. Johnson. We'll send a police officer right away.
Judy: Thank you. Good-bye.

3. Operator: 911 Emergency.
Mr. Sato: Hello. I need help. There's a fire in my garage.
Operator: What's your name?
Mr. Sato: Gary Sato.
Operator: What's your address?
Mr. Sato: 3757 Hill Street.
Operator: OK. Stay away from your garage, Mr. Sato. We'll send a fire truck right away.
Mr. Sato: Thank you. Good-bye.

4. Operator: 911 Emergency.
Mrs. Sato: Hello. I need help. My daughter fell down the stairs. She's unconscious.
Operator: What's your name?
Mrs. Sato: Kitty Sato.
Operator: What's your address?
Mrs. Sato: 3757 Hill Street.
Operator: OK. Don't move your daughter, Mrs. Sato. Cover her with a blanket and keep her warm. We'll send an ambulance right away.
Mrs. Sato: Thank you. Good-bye.

UNIT 22, P. 140

9. Before you listen to each speaker, read the sentences with your teacher. Then listen to the speaker and circle the letter of what to say next.

1. There was a car accident, and a man is hurt.
2. Is he unconscious?
3. My son just drank some diarrhea medicine.
4. How much medicine did he drink?
5. What happened?
6. Is anyone hurt?
7. Someone is trying to get into my neighbor's house.

8. Is your neighbor at home?
9. There's a fire in my kitchen.
10. My wife is unconscious.

UNIT 23, P. 148

10. Listen to other people talking to the doctor. Circle the problem each person has. Then write when it started.

1. Doctor: How are you, Mrs. Sato?
Mrs. Sato: Not so good. I'm congested, and I cough a lot at night.
Doctor: Hmm. When did this problem start?
Mrs. Sato: One week ago. What can I do about it?
Doctor: First, I'll listen inside your chest. You may have an infection in your lungs.

2. Doctor: How are you, Susan?
Susan: Not so good. I have diarrhea.
Doctor: Hmm. When did this problem start?
Susan: About two weeks ago. What can I do about it?
Doctor: First, we'll do some tests. You may have an infection in your intestine.

3. Doctor: How are you, Judy?
Judy: Not so good. It hurts when I urinate.
Doctor: Hmm. When did this problem start?
Judy: Three days ago. What can I do about it?
Doctor: First, we'll do some tests. You may have a kidney infection.

4. Doctor: How are you, Sam?
Sam: Not so good. My eyes are yellow.
Doctor: Hmm. When did they start to look yellow?
Sam: About five weeks ago. What can I do about it?
Doctor: First, I'll examine your eyes. You may have a problem with your liver.

5. Doctor: How are you, Mr. Sato?
Mr. Sato: Not so good. I can't breathe well, and I cough all the time.
Doctor: Hmm. When did this problem start?
Mr. Sato: Six months ago. What can I do about it?
Doctor: First, we'll do some tests. You may have a heart problem.

Listen again. Check *yes* if the people are going to have tests and check *no* if they aren't. Then circle the doctor's diagnosis.

UNIT 24, P. 152

3. Listen and complete the sentences.

1. Yesterday the Satos <u>bought plane tickets</u> for their trip.
2. Judy is <u>feeling lonely</u> right now.
3. Carlos <u>weighed himself</u> yesterday.
4. Tomorrow the Satos are going to <u>lie in the sun</u>.
5. Two days ago, Judy <u>packed her suitcase</u>.

6. The Satos <u>made reservations</u> for their trip two days ago.
7. Carlos is going to <u>go on a diet</u> tomorrow.
8. Right now the Satos <u>are flying</u> to Hawaii.

UNIT 24, P. 155

8. Listen to other people making airline reservations. Write the number of people in each party. Then write the dates and times of departure and arrival for each flight.

1. **Travel Agent:** Pacific Travel.
   Judy: Hello. I'd like to make a plane reservation to Chicago.
   Travel Agent: Your name, please?
   Judy: Judy Johnson.
   Travel Agent: How many are in your party, Ms. Johnson?
   Judy: One. Just me.
   Travel Agent: When do you want to leave?
   Judy: December 22nd.
   Travel Agent: And when do you want to return?
   Judy: January 3rd.
   Travel Agent: All right. On December 22nd, Flight 72 on World Airlines leaves Los Angeles at 8:15 A.M. and arrives in Chicago at 2:20 P.M. Is that OK?
   Judy: Leave 8:15. Arrive 2:20. That's fine.
   Travel Agent: On January 3rd, Flight 84 leaves Chicago at 10:00 A.M. and arrives in Los Angeles at 12:05 P.M. Is that OK?
   Judy: Leave 10:00. Arrive 12:05. Yes, that's OK.
   Travel Agent: All right, Ms. Johnson. You can pick up your tickets anytime.
   Judy: Thank you. Good-bye.

2. **Travel Agent:** Pacific Travel.
   Susan: Hello. I'd like to make a plane reservation to New York.
   Travel Agent: Your name, please?
   Susan: Susan Gomez.
   Travel Agent: How many are in your party, Ms. Gomez?
   Susan: Four. Two adults and two children.
   Travel Agent: When do you want to leave?
   Susan: May 31st.
   Travel Agent: And when do you want to return?
   Susan: June 14th.
   Travel Agent: All right. On May 31st, Flight 1062 on World Airlines leaves Los Angeles at 7:45 A.M. and arrives in New York at 4:10 P.M. Is that OK?
   Susan: Leave 7:45. Arrive 4:10. That's fine.
   Travel Agent: On June 14th, Flight 1037 leaves New York at 8:50 A.M. and arrives in Los Angeles at 11:30. Is that OK?
   Susan: Leave 8:50. Arrive 11:30. Yes, that's OK.
   Travel Agent: All right, Ms. Gomez. You can pick up your tickets anytime.
   Susan: Thank you. Good-bye.

3. **Travel Agent:** Atlantic Travel.
   Marco: Hello. I'd like to make a plane reservation to Los Angeles.
   Travel Agent: Your name, please?
   Marco: Marco Gomez.
   Travel Agent: How many are in your party, Mr. Gomez?
   Marco: Three. Two adults and one child.
   Travel Agent: When do you want to leave?
   Marco: April 1st.
   Travel Agent: And when do you want to return?
   Marco: April 8th.
   Travel Agent: All right. On April 1st, Flight 404 on World Airlines leaves Miami at 1:05 P.M. and arrives in Los Angeles at 4:20. Is that OK?
   Marco: Leave 1:05. Arrive 4:20. That's fine.
   Travel Agent: On April 8th, Flight 275 leaves Los Angeles at 8:00 A.M. and arrives in Miami at 4:35 P.M. Is that OK?
   Marco: Leave 8:00. Arrive 4:35. Yes, that's OK.
   Travel Agent: All right, Mr. Gomez. You can pick up your tickets anytime.
   Marco: Thank you. Good-bye.

4. **Travel Agent:** Pacific Travel.
   Tran: Hello. I'd like to make a plane reservation to Hong Kong.
   Travel Agent: Your name, please?
   Tran: Tran Ng.
   Travel Agent: How many are in your party, Mr. Ng?
   Tran: One. Just me.
   Travel Agent: When do you want to leave?
   Tran: September 25th.
   Travel Agent: And when do you want to return?
   Tran: October 26th.
   Travel Agent: All right. On September 25th, Flight 1122 on World Airlines leaves Los Angeles at 10:15 A.M. and arrives in Hong Kong at 3:45 P.M. Is that OK?
   Tran: Leave 10:15. Arrive 3:45. That's fine.
   Travel Agent: On October 26th, Flight 1208 leaves Hong Kong at 6:00 A.M. and arrives in Los Angeles at 11:55 P.M. Is that OK?
   Tran: Leave 6:00. Arrive 11:55. Yes, that's OK.
   Travel Agent: All right, Mr. Ng. You can pick up your tickets anytime.
   Tran: Thank you. Good-bye.

5. **Travel Agent:** Pacific Travel.
   Ken: Hello. I'd like to make a plane reservation to San Francisco.
   Travel Agent: Your name, please?
   Ken: Ken Wong.
   Travel Agent: How many are in your party, Mr. Wong?
   Ken: Two. My girlfriend, Judy Johnson, and me.
   Travel Agent: When do you want to leave?
   Ken: June 28th.

Travel Agent: And when do you want to return?
Ken: July 5th.
Travel Agent: All right. On June 28th, Flight 79 on World Airlines leaves Los Angeles at 9:50 A.M. and arrives in San Francisco at 11:15. Is that OK?
Ken: Leave 9:50. Arrive 11:15. That's fine.
Travel Agent: On July 5th, Flight 86 leaves San Francisco at 6:15 A.M. and arrives in Los Angeles at 7:40. OK?
Ken: Leave 6:15 A.M. Arrive 7:40. Yes, that's OK.
Judy: What?!! Six fifteen in the morning is too early!
Ken: Just a minute, Judy. Excuse me. Is there a later flight on July 5th?
Travel Agent: No, I'm sorry. All the other flights are sold out.
Ken: Well, then, I guess we'll take the 6:15 flight.
Judy: Oh, no! I never get up before 7:30!
Ken: It's just *one* day, Judy!
Travel Agent: All right, Mr. Wong. You can pick up your tickets anytime.
Ken: Thank you. Good-bye.
Judy: Six fifteen in the morning?!! What kind of vacation is that?

UNIT 25, P. 158

3. Listen and complete the sentences.

1. I want you to <u>peel</u> these <u>apples</u>.
2. Please use a <u>sponge</u> to wash the windows.
3. I want you to <u>paint</u> those <u>walls</u> now.
4. Use glue to <u>make</u> those <u>boxes</u>.
5. Could you please paint the <u>whole room</u>?
6. I want you to use <u>blue</u> thread on those <u>buttons</u>. OK?
7. Would you please make <u>one dozen</u> boxes?
8. I want you to use a <u>paintbrush</u> on those <u>walls</u>.

UNIT 25, P. 161

9. Listen to employees asking about job benefits. Check the benefits each employee will get. If the employee gets paid vacation, write how much time. If the employee gets paid sick days, write how many.

1. **Boss:** Do you have any questions about benefits, Eva?
   Eva: Yes. Do I get health and dental insurance?
   Boss: You get health insurance after one month, but we have no dental insurance plan yet.
   Eva: I see. How about vacations and holidays?
   Boss: You get two weeks' paid vacation every year. Of course, we're closed on holidays. So you get paid holidays too.
   Eva: OK. How about sick days?
   Boss: You get ten paid sick days per year.

2. **Boss:** Do you have any questions about benefits, Les?
   Les: Yes. Do I get health and dental insurance?
   Boss: I'm sorry, but our part-time employees don't get health or dental insurance.
   Les: I see. How about vacations and holidays?
   Boss: You get one week of paid vacation every year. We're open on most holidays, so there are no paid holidays.
   Les: OK. How about sick days?
   Boss: You get twelve paid sick days per year.

3. **Boss:** Do you have any questions about benefits, Ruth?
   Ruth: Yes. Do I get health and dental insurance?
   Boss: Yes, you do. You get both health and dental insurance, and our health plans are very good.
   Ruth: I see. How about vacations and holidays?
   Boss: You get two weeks' paid vacation every year. You get paid holidays too.
   Ruth: OK. How about sick days?
   Boss: You get one paid sick day per month.

4. **Boss:** Do you have any questions about benefits, Sam?
   Sam: Yes. Do I get health and dental insurance?
   Boss: You get health insurance after three months, but we have no dental insurance plan.
   Sam: I see. How about vacations and holidays?
   Boss: You can go on vacation when you want to, but we don't give our employees any vacation pay. But of course we're closed on holidays, so you get ten paid holidays per year.
   Sam: OK. How about sick days?
   Boss: You also get ten paid sick days per year.

5. **Boss:** Do you have any questions about benefits, Lisa?
   Lisa: Yes. Do I get health and dental insurance?
   Boss: I'm sorry, but our part-time employees don't get health or dental insurance.
   Lisa: I see. How about vacations and holidays?
   Boss: There is no paid vacation for part-time employees. But we're closed on holidays, so you get twelve paid holidays per year.
   Lisa: OK. How about sick days?
   Boss: You get six paid sick days per year.

6. **Boss:** I hope you'll like working here at the candy shop, Ivan. Do you have any questions?
   Ivan: Yes. I'd like to know about benefits. Do I get health insurance?
   Boss: Yes, you do. We have a very good health plan.
   Ivan: I see. How about vacations and holidays?
   Boss: You get one week of paid vacation. You get paid holidays too.
   Ivan: OK. How about sick days?
   Boss: You get ten paid sick days a year. And you can have all the candy you want—candy is free for our employees.
   Ivan: Free candy?! Wow! But wait a minute. Do I get dental insurance?

Boss: Dental insurance? No, I'm sorry.
We don't have a dental plan.
Ivan: Ohhhh. I guess I won't eat much candy then!

UNIT 26, P. 165

3. Listen and complete the sentences.

1. When you carry glass, you <u>should always</u> use gloves.
2. That's very heavy. You <u>might hurt</u> your back.
3. That's not safe. You should always <u>carry scissors</u> pointing down.
4. Be careful! Don't smoke there! You might <u>start a fire</u>.
5. You should always wear <u>safety glasses</u> around machines.
6. Don't touch those wires! You might <u>get a shock</u>.
7. That's not safe. You <u>should never</u> bend down to pick up something heavy.
8. Be careful of your hands. You should always <u>use gloves</u> when you hold glass.

UNIT 26, P. 166

6. Now look at the pictures and read the signs with your teacher. Then listen to the conversations and write the number of each conversation under the correct picture.

1. **A:** Watch it!
   B: Huh?
   A: You shouldn't touch that wall.
   B: How come?
   A: It has wet paint. See the sign?
   B: Oh, yeah. Thanks.

2. **A:** Don't go inside that door.
   B: Why not?
   A: The sign says "No Admittance." You can't go in there.
   B: Oh, I see.

3. **A:** Excuse me. Where's the women's restroom?
   B: It's down the hall to the left. But you can't use it now.
   A: Why not?
   B: It's out of order.
   A: Oh, I see.

4. **A:** Hey, Ivan. Slow down!
   B: How come?
   A: The floor is wet. See the sign?
   B: Oh, yeah. Thanks.

5. **A:** Excuse me. You can't smoke here.
   B: Why not?
   A: There's oil in there. It's flammable. There might be a fire.
   B: Oh, yeah. Thanks for telling me.

6. **A:** Please move those boxes away from the door.
   B: How come?
   A: That's a fire exit. You can't block the doorway.
   B: Oh, I see.

UNIT 27, P. 170

3. Listen and complete the sentences.

1. I like walking on the streets because they're so <u>clean</u>.
2. The downtown part of my hometown is really <u>busy</u>.
3. I like the people there because they are <u>friendly</u>.
4. You have to hold on to your hat because it's often <u>windy</u>!
5. Everyone carries umbrellas there because it's so <u>rainy</u>.
6. You get tired walking there because the town is <u>hilly</u>.
7. It's OK to walk there at night because it's <u>safe</u>.
8. There's no problem sleeping there because it's always <u>quiet</u>.

UNIT 27, P. 174

10. Susan and Carlos are inviting friends to do things this weekend. Listen to their conversations and write the missing words. Then practice the conversations with your teacher.

1. **Susan:** Say, Betsy, would you like to <u>go shopping</u> with me this weekend?
   Betsy: Sure. I'd love to.
   Susan: Great. Which day is <u>better</u> for you, Saturday or Sunday?
   Betsy: <u>Saturday</u> is better for me.
   Susan: OK.
   Betsy: What time <u>should</u> we go?
   Susan: How about <u>1:00</u>?
   Betsy: That sounds fine. I'll look forward to it.

2. **Carlos:** Say, Tom, would you and Marsha like to <u>come over</u> for dinner this weekend?
   Tom: We'd love to, but we <u>can't</u>. This weekend we're <u>going</u> out of town.
   Carlos: Oh, well. Maybe some other time.
   Tom: Yeah. Thanks anyway.

UNIT 28, P. 176

3. Listen and complete the sentences.

1. Everyone takes pictures there because it's so <u>scenic</u>.
2. I don't like to take the buses there. They're too <u>crowded</u>.
3. The museums in my hometown are really <u>interesting</u>.
4. I don't like walking there at night because it's <u>dangerous</u>!
5. Everybody knows about my city. It's very <u>famous</u>.
6. All the buildings in my hometown are new. It's a <u>modern</u> city.
7. You have to be rich to live here because it's so <u>expensive</u>.
8. There are lots of places to eat out or go dancing. It's a <u>fun</u> city.

UNIT 28, P. 178

7. Listen to other people giving compliments. Circle what they are talking about. Then write how it is different from the old one.

1. A: I really like your new house.
   B: Thank you.
   A: It's so beautiful. Does it have a basement?
   B: Yes, it does. This house is bigger than our old one.

2. A: I really like your new kitchen.
   B: Thank you.
   A: It's so sunny. Is it easy to work in?
   B: Yes, it is. This kitchen is more modern than my old one.

3. A: I really like your new coat.
   B: Thank you.
   A: It looks so nice on you. Was it expensive?
   B: No, it was on sale. This coat was cheaper than my old one.

4. A: I really like your new car.
   B: Thank you.
   A: It's so cute. Is it easy to park?
   B: Yes, it is. This car is smaller than my old one.

5. A: I really like your new boyfriend.
   B: Thank you.
   A: He's so funny. Is he interesting to talk to?
   B: Yes, he is. He's more interesting than my old boyfriend.
   A: That's good. Your old boyfriend wasn't very good at conversation, was he?
   B: What do you mean? *Your* boyfriend doesn't say much either!
   A: Wait a minute! At least *my* boyfriend is cute!
   B: What?! My boyfriend is cuter than yours!
   A: No way! My boyfriend is cuter than yours, and he's nicer, too!
   B: No, he isn't! My boyfriend is definitely nicer than yours, *and* he's taller.
   A: Well, my boyfriend has more money than yours.

Teacher's Notes

BEFORE UNIT 1

Follow-up activities for vocabulary from pages 1-2

1. Write the following cues on the chalkboard:

name	day	time	age

As you point to the individual cues, say:

Ask the question.   or   **Answer the question.**

Examples: Point to **name**; say, "Ask the question."
Student responds: "What's your name?"

Point to **name**; say, "Answer the question."
Student responds: "My name is _____."

Do not correct for accuracy. The point of the practice is appropriateness of response.

2. Say one of the following three cues:

1, 2, 3, . . .   A, B, C, . . .
Monday, Tuesday, Wednesday. . . .

Then say one of these commands:

Repeat.   Continue.   Go on.   Next.

Examples: Say, "One, two, three . . . Repeat."➡
Student responds: "One, two, three."

Say, "One, two, three . . . Continue."➡
Student responds: "Four, five, six, . . . "

3. Write the following sentences on the chalkboard:

Please look at your book.
Write your name on your paper.
They is my friends.
What is your name?

Point to individual sentences or words on the chalkboard as you say the commands or ask the questions given below.

Examples: Point to **Please look at your book**; ask, "What's the first word?"
➡ Student responds: "Please."

Point to **They is my friends**; say, "Correct the mistake."
➡ Student responds: "They are my friends."

<u>Commands and questions:</u>
Say the word/sentence.
How many words/sentences?
What's the first word/sentence?
What's the last word/sentence?
Correct the mistake.

4. Now go back and practice the commands and questions in random order.

Follow-up activities for vocabulary from pages 3-4.

Write the following words on the chalkboard:

big   little   unhappy   begin   fast   book   boys

Point to individual words on the chalkboard as you ask various questions given below.

Examples: Point to **big**; ask, "What does this mean?"
➡Student responds: "Large."

Point to **little**; ask, "How do you pronounce this?"
➡Student responds: "Little."

Point to **unhappy**; ask, "What's the opposite?"
➡Student responds: "Happy."

Point to **begin**; ask, "How do you spell this?"
➡Student responds: "B-e-g-i-n."

Point to **fast**; say, "Give an example."
➡Student responds: "Airplane."

Point to **little**; ask, "How many syllables?"
➡Student responds: "Two."

Point to **book**; ask, "Singular or plural?"
➡Student responds: "Singular."

Questions:
What does this mean?   (What's the meaning?)
How do you pronounce this? (What's the pronunciation?)
How do you spell this?   (What's the spelling?)
What's the opposite?
Give an example.
How many syllables/vowels/consonants?
What's the first vowel/consonant?
Singular or plural?

Units 1-28

Please read Presenting New Vocabulary with Pictures (page viii) before reading the following notes.

This section includes, for Units 1-28, questions to ask while presenting the pictures on the first page, and a sample of how the presentation of the page might start out. Since actual classroom presentations will be interactive, and therefore guided by students' responses, they will not follow these models exactly. That is, these are not scripts, but rather guides from which to draw ideas for creating natural and personalized presentations suited to your students.

Specific teaching notes are also given for selected units. You are urged to read these notes before beginning a new unit, although with time you may find it unnecessary to refer to the sample presentations.

UNIT 1: What's Your Name? (page 7)

Teaching note: This unit is designed to provide: (1) a review of formulaic personal questions which ESL students generally study at the literacy level, and (2) a vehicle for you and your students to get to know each other. Look at page 8 while presenting page 7. Ask each question of several students and encourage class members to expand on their answers without focusing on grammatical accuracy at this point. Before beginning the pairwork (Activity 4), have volunteers model the seven questions as the students look at the pictures.

Sample presentation, Pictures 1 and 2: name and country

Today we're going to talk about ourselves, so we can get to know each other. What's your name [pointing to picture 1]? . . . It's Tran. Is that your first name or your last name? . . . Your first name. And your last name? . . . Nham. Tran Nham. It's nice to have you in class. Where are you from, Tran [pointing to picture 2]? . . . You're from Vietnam. What city are you from? . . . Oh, a little village by the beach. Nobody knows it. What's the name of your village? . . . You're right. I *haven't* heard of it. People say that the beach in Vietnam is very beautiful. . . . It is? How many years did you live in Vietnam? . . . Twenty. I see. Now, how about *you*? What's your name? . . .

UNIT 2: What's That? What's It For? (page 11)

Teaching note: When you ask what the items on page 11 are used for, students' responses needn't be restricted to those listed on page 12. The captions on page 12 are for students' reference, but appropriate variations or expansions are to be encouraged.

Ask questions like the following to present the pictures:

• What's this (called)?

• What's this (used) for?

• Do you have a _____ at home?

• Where do you keep your_____?

• What color is your _____?

• Do you ever use a _____? At work or at home?

• How big is a _____?

The Pictures

1. broom—sweep the floor
2. mops—clean the floor
3. pail—hold water
4. sponges—wash dishes
5. detergent—wash dishes
6. towels—dry things
7. iron—press clothes
8. gloves—protect your hands
9. rulers—measure things
10. scale—weigh things
11. light bulbs—light the room
12. wastebasket—throw things away
13. hammer—fix things
14. screwdrivers—fix things
15. pliers—fix things
16. scissors—cut things

Sample presentation, Picture 1: broom

Today we're going to talk about things we use at work or at home. What's this picture of? . . . Well, is it a pencil or a broom? . . . Yes, it's a broom. How many parts to a broom? . . . Yes, a broom has two parts [pointing]. How big is a broom? This big? This big [indicating with hands]? . . . Yes, about this big. Do you have a broom in your house, Dac? . . . You do? Where do you keep your broom? . . . In the kitchen. And what's a broom used for? . . . Yes, it's for sweeping the floor. Where's the floor, everybody? . . . That's right [pointing]. Do you sweep the floor at home, Dac? . . . Oh, what a good husband! Marco, what color is the broom in your house? You don't know? My goodness, I'd hate to see the floor in your house! . . . Oh, I see. Your wife does the sweeping. Well, OK then. . . .

UNIT 3: Where's the Pail? (page 17)

Teaching note: Look at page 18 while presenting page 17. Read each statement, pointing to the items in the picture and clarifying the highlighted expression from the text. Then ask about other items in the picture (and in the classroom) to elicit answers using the same expression.

Sample presentation, Expression 1: to the right/left of

Today we're going to talk about shelves. What are shelves? Are there any in this room? . . . Yes, [pointing] those are shelves. How many shelves are there? . . . Four shelves. And what are shelves used for? . . . Yes, for keeping things. What do we keep on those shelves? . . . Books. Any shelves in your house, Natalia? . . . Yes? Where are they? . . . In your kitchen. Are there shelves where any of you work? Raise your hands. . . . I see lots of you have shelves at work. And sometimes we need to say where things are on shelves. Look at these shelves now; look at the sponges and the pail [pointing with both hands]. Is the pail *over* the sponges? . . . No. It's . . . [emphasizing each word] *to the right of* the sponges. How many words was that [showing four fingers]? . . . Yes, four words: *to the right of*. And where are the sponges, then? . . . Yes, to the left of the pail. Now, look at the calendar and map on our wall [pointing]. Where's the map? . . . To the right of the calendar. And the door and window over there. Where's the window? . . . To the left of the door.

UNIT 4: Where's Judy? What's She Doing? (page 23)

Teaching note: When you ask what the people on page 23 are doing at the various businesses, students' responses needn't be restricted to those listed on page 24. The captions on page 24 are for students' reference, but appropriate variations or expansions are to be encouraged.

Ask questions like the following to present the pictures:

- What is this (place)?
- Who's at the _____?
- What's he/she doing at the _____?
- Where do *you* _____?
- How far is your _____ from your house?
- Is there a _____ near school?

The Pictures

1. department store—buy clothes
2. bakery—buy bread and cake
3. hardware store—buy tools
4. grocery store (supermarket)—buy food
5. auto repair shop—get the car fixed
6. barber shop *or* beauty salon— get a haircut
7. bank—get cash
8. furniture store—buy furniture
9. toy store—buy toys
10. thrift shop (secondhand store)—buy used things
11. drugstore (pharmacy)—buy medicine
12. parking lot—park the car

Sample presentation, Picture 1: department store

Today we're going to talk about businesses. Look at this picture. Where is Judy? . . . Well, where do you buy clothes? . . . Yes, at a department store. What are some department stores in town? . . . Yes, Macy's . . . .And Woolworth's. Those are both department stores . . . That's right, Mei. You can also buy other things at department stores. Do you live near a department store, Tho? . . . You live near Woolworth's? What about you, Angela? Is there a department store near your house? . . . There isn't. Now, back to our picture. Who's at the department store? . . . Yes, Judy is. And what's she doing there? . . . Well, is she buying food? . . . No. She's buying clothes.

UNIT 5: Where's Susan Going? (page 29)

Teaching note: During the presentation and conversation practice in this unit, students will be asked a question whose answer is not given in the book: *Why* is this person going to this place? Here, as in other places indicated in the book, the aim is to reinforce the new language—and have some fun—by engaging in free speculation.

For each picture, first ask the following two questions:

- Where's this person going/walking?
- Why is he/she going _____? (free speculation)

Then demonstrate or elicit other examples of the prepositions being taught, as in the sample presentation below.

The Pictures

1. across the street
2. up the hill (to the top of the hill)
3. down the hill (to the bottom of the hill)
4. down the street
5. around the corner
6. around the block
7. along the river
8. through the window
9. through the park
10. across the bridge
11. toward the window
12. away from the window

Sample presentation, Picture 1: across the street

Today we're going to talk about people walking and driving places. First, let's look at Susan. Where's Susan going? . . . Is she walking across the room? . . . No. She's walking across the street. By the way, what do we always have to do *before* we walk across the street? . . . Yes, we need to wait for the green light. And look both ways. Now, *why* do you think Susan is going across the street? Any ideas? . . . Yes, maybe she sees her friend on the other side. Any other ideas why she's walking across the street? . . . Yes, maybe she's going to the store. Why else might she be going across the street? . . .

UNIT 6: Where Was Carlos during the Earthquake? (page 33)

Teaching note: The background for the presentation is an earthquake that happened "yesterday at 2:47 P.M." Ask where each of the people on page 33 was at the time of the quake and what he or she was doing. As in Unit 4, students may suggest other activities that the various people were doing at the different places, and this is to be encouraged.

Ask questions like the following to present the pictures:

- What is this (place)?
- What was this person doing at the _____?
- What else can we do at a _____?
- Is there a _____ near your house?
- How often do you go to the _____?
- Are there many _____ in our city?

The Pictures

1. library—read a magazine
2. bus station—meet a friend
3. day-care center—take a nap
4. clinic—wait for the doctor
5. hospital—visit a friend
6. playground—play basketball

7. police station—talk about a problem
8. airport—leave on a trip
9. post office—buy stamps
10. employment office—ask about jobs
11. museum—look at pictures
12. church—sing

Sample presentation, Picture 1: Carlos reading a magazine at the library

Well, class, I have some sad news. Yesterday, in Carlos's city, there was a big earthquake at 2:47 in the afternoon. Do you know what an earthquake is? . . . Yes, [indicating with hands and body] it's when buildings and houses shake. Do you like earthquakes? . . . No. They're scary, aren't they? Did any of you have an earthquake in your country? . . . Yes, Anita. The earthquake in Mexico City was very big. . . . And you say there are always earthquakes in Japan, Yoshiko? I wouldn't like that! Now, let's look where everyone was during yesterday's earthquake. Where was Carlos? . . . This is a building with lots of books. . . . Yes, it's a library. Carlos was at the library. Is there a library near school? . . . Yes, there's a library on Stockton Street. And is there a library near your house? . . . There's a library near your house, Ulises? Do you ever go to the library? . . . You do. Now, what do you think Carlos was doing at the library yesterday? . . . Yes, maybe he was reading a book. Or, do you know what a magazine is? . . . Yes, a magazine comes out every week, or every month. Does anyone have a magazine with them now? . . . Show it to the class, Ana. What's your magazine about? . . . Oh, it's a magazine about movie stars! Anyone else read magazines? . . .

UNIT 7: Is There a Listening Lab at Our School? (page 39)

Ask questions like the following to present the pictures:

- What do people do at a _____?
  or What's a _____ for?
- Is there a/Are there_____ in our school?
- Where is/are the_____ in our school?
- Where else can we find _____ ?
- Do you ever use the _____ in our school?

The Pictures

1. listening lab
2. typing classes
3. library
4. computers
5. counselors' office
6. tape recorders
7. copy machine
8. night classes
9. student lounge
10. vending machines
11. bookstore
12. emergency exits

Sample presentation, Picture 1: listening lab

Today we're going to talk about things we find at schools. Do you know what this is? . . . Yes, it's a listening lab. What do people do at a listening lab? . . . Yes, students listen to tapes. Is there a listening lab at our school? . . . Yes, there is. Where is our listening lab? . . . It's across the hall, in Room 209. Does anybody ever use the listening lab here? . . . You do, Alex? What do you use the listening lab for? . . . For listening to the tape of our book. Does anyone else use the listening lab? . . . You do, Salvador? When do you use it? . . .

UNIT 8: How Many Rooms Are There in the Apartment? (page 45)

Teaching note: Introduce this unit by telling students they will be practicing questions people ask when looking for an apartment. Look at page 46 as you present page 45, asking the question that is given beside each picture. Ask students the questions about their own apartments, reinforcing the target vocabulary by having them elaborate on their answers, and then ask if they can make the questions. During the presentation, and again before beginning the pairwork (Activity 3), have volunteers model the questions as the students look at the pictures.

Sample presentation for page 45, Picture 1: How many rooms are there in the apartment?

Today we're going to talk about the questions we need to ask when we look for an apartment. First, we ask [pointing to the first picture] how many . . . yes; how many rooms in the apartment. Ruben, how many rooms are in your apartment? . . . Four rooms? What are they? . . . I see. And you, Huang? How many rooms are there in your apartment? . . . Two rooms. You live alone. Now, can you make the question? "How many . . . ?" You want to try, Pedro? . . . Very good. Anyone else want to try? . . .

Presenting page 49 (Activity 6)

Look at page 49 (or an OHT of the page) while presenting the pictures. For each of pictures 1-5, ask students:

> Are there many_____ in your house/neighborhood?

(There is no new vocabulary represented by these pictures.)

The vocabulary represented by pictures 6-10 (except for *furniture*) has not yet appeared in the book, so first clarify the meaning of each. Then ask students:

> Is there much_____ in your house/neighborhood?

UNIT 9: What's Wrong with the Refrigerator? (page 51)

Presenting page 51

Look at page 52 while presenting page 51. Ask, "What's the problem here?" about each numbered item in the pictures, eliciting the statements that appear on page 52. (Students may offer other, equally acceptable descriptions of the problem; these should be encouraged.)

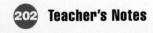

Reinforce the target vocabulary by relating it to the students' lives.

Sample presentation for page 51, Picture 1: The refrigerator isn't working

Today we're going to talk about problems we sometimes have in our homes. Let's look at the first picture. A lot of things aren't working in this apartment. What does that mean, "aren't working"? . . . Yes, it means they're broken. . . . Right; it's the same as "don't work." What isn't working in this picture? [pointing] . . . The refrigerator isn't working. Who has a refrigerator in their house? . . . I see everyone does. And where is your refrigerator? . . . In the kitchen. What's the refrigerator used for? . . . Yes, keeping food cold. Did you ever have a problem with your refrigerator not working? . . . You did, Thuy? . . . You were away on vacation for a month? My goodness! Yes, I can imagine the smell. What did you do about it? . . .

Presenting page 55

Look at page 56 while presenting page 55. Ask two questions about each of the numbered details in the picture:

- What's wrong here? (Elicit the statements that appear on page 56.)
- Why is this a problem? (Let students answer in their own words, helping them if necessary.)

Reinforce the new language by relating it to the students' homes.

Sample presentation for page 55, Item 1: poison on the table

Today we're going to talk about being safe at home. What is "safe"? . . . Yes, it means you don't hurt yourself. For example, do children play in the street? . . . No; that's not safe. They can get hurt. Now, let's look at this picture. Where is this? . . . Yes, it's a kitchen. And what's this on the table? [pointing] . . . Is it milk or poison? . . . Yes, it's poison. What is poison? . . . It makes you sick if you eat it. . . . Maybe you will die. How do you know it's poison? . . . By the picture [pointing to skull and crossbones]. What's an example of poison? . . . Well, is gasoline a poison? . . . Yes. What else? . . . Yes, bleach is a poison. Now, where is this poison? . . . It's on the table. Is that safe? . . . Of course not. It's . . . yes, it's dangerous. *Dangerous* is the opposite of *safe*. Why is this dangerous? . . . Because a child might drink it. Do you keep poisons on the table in your kitchen, Chun? . . . Good! I'm glad to hear it!

UNIT 10: Do You Ever Use a Credit Card? (page 65)

Teaching note: When you ask about the first picture during the presentation, write *Do you ever . . . ?* on the chalkboard and explain that this means "Do you sometimes . . . ?" (Then erase the words from the chalkboard.) If necessary, remind students of the two answers to this question: "Yes, I do" and "No, I don't," and tell them that we can also answer, "No, never."

Ask questions like the following to present the pictures:

- Do you ever _____?
- How often do you _____?
- Where/When do you _____?
- Why do you _____?

The Pictures

1. **use a credit card**
2. **worry about money**
3. **write checks**
4. **shop at thrift stores**
5. **buy red socks**
6. **go to garage sales**
7. **shop at department stores**
8. **borrow money**
9. **buy flowers**
10. **lose your money**
11. **return clothes**
12. **steal things**

Sample presentation, Picture 1: use a credit card

Now let me ask you: Do you ever use a credit card? Well, first of all, what is a credit card? Who has one? Hold it up. . . . Joaquín has a VISA card. That's a credit card . . . And Elena has a Mastercard. That's a credit card, too. Now *when* do you use a credit card? . . . Yes, when you go shopping. And *why* do you use a credit card? . . . Yes, when you don't have money with you . . . Or you don't want to carry money. So, Elena, where do *you* use your credit card? . . . At Macy's, when you buy clothes. And what do you have to show when you use your credit card? . . . .Yes, you show ID . . . .And you sign your name. Joaquín, how often do you use your credit card? . . . Oh, not very much. You like to pay cash.

UNIT 11: What Does Ken Do on Weeknights? (page 65)

Teaching note: Before beginning the presentation, remind students that we use *does* and *do* to ask about things that people *usually* or *sometimes* (i.e., habitually) do.

Ask questions like the following to present the pictures:

- What does (Ken) usually do on weeknights?
- Do you ever _____?
- Do you enjoy _____ing?
- How often do you _____?
- Where do you _____?
- Who do you _____with?

The Pictures

Ken
weeknights—reads books
Friday night— plays cards
Saturday— plays soccer
Sunday—goes to church

Judy
weeknights—relaxes
Friday night—goes dancing
Saturday—runs in the park
Sunday—doesn't do anything

Linda and Paul
weeknights—do homework
Friday night— watch TV
Saturday—play with (their) friends
Sunday—don't do anything

Sample presentation, Picture 1: read books

Today we're going to talk about what people do in their leisure time. What is "leisure time"? . . . Yes, it's our free time. When do we have leisure time? . . . On Sunday . . . After work . . . During vacation. Now, look at these letters [pointing to *MTWTh*]. What are they? . . . Yes, Monday, Tuesday, Wednesday, Thursday. Daytime or nighttime [pointing to the moon]? . . . Nighttime. These are what we call "weeknights." What are weeknights, then? . . . Right. Now, let's talk about Ken. What does he do on week- nights? . . . He reads books. Any idea what kind of books he reads? . . . Maybe adventure stories . . . Maybe love stories. Do any of you read books on weeknights? . . .

UNIT 12: What Does Judy Do? (page 71)

Teaching note: When you ask what the various people do in their jobs, students' responses needn't be restricted to those listed on page 72. The captions on page 72 are for students' reference, but appropriate variations or expansions are to be encouraged.

Ask questions like the following to present the pictures:

• What is this person's job?
• Where does a _____ work?
• What does a _____ do?
• Do you know a _____?
• Is any of you a _____?
• What does a _____ wear?

The Pictures

1. secretary/receptionist—type letters and answer phones
2. construction worker—build houses and buildings
3. stock clerk—put things on shelves
4. seamstress—sew clothes
5. factory worker—work in a factory
6. mail carrier—deliver mail
7. fire fighter—put out fires
8. police officer—protect citizens
9. plumber—fix pipes
10. mechanic—repair cars and machines
11. janitor—clean offices and buildings
12. electrician—work with electricity
13. cashier—take money and give change
14. waitress/waiter—serve food
15. security guard—guard stores and banks
16. dentist—take care of our teeth

Sample presentation, Picture 1: secretary/receptionist

Today we're going to talk about people's jobs. Look at Judy. What does she do? . . . She's a secretary. Also, she helps people who visit the office. Do you know what we call that person? . . . Well, is she a teacher or a receptionist? . . . She's a receptionist. Can you say that? . . . Now, where does a secretary or receptionist work? . . . In an office. And what does a secretary or receptionist do? . . . Yes, a secretary types letters. What else? . . . Yes, a receptionist answers the telephone. What else? . . . Yes, a receptionist answers your questions when you go to the office. Now, is any of you a secretary or receptionist, or were you in your country? . . . You were, Olga? What did you do as a receptionist? . . .

UNIT 13: Can You Drive a Truck? (page 77)

Teaching note: If necessary during the presentation, help students with the answers "Yes, I can" and "No, I can't."

Ask questions like the following to present the pictures:

• Can you _____?
• Can anyone in your family _____?
• Do you ever _____ at work?
• How often do you _____?
• Where/When did you learn to _____?
• Do you enjoy _____ing?

The Pictures

1. drive a truck
2. use a calculator
3. type
4. read maps
5. use a computer
6. repair machines
7. use hand tools
8. use electric tools
9. alter clothes
10. use a cash register
11. change a tire
12. fool your boss

Sample presentation, Picture 1: drive a truck

Today we're going to talk about things we can or can't do. Sergio, can you drive a truck? . . . No, you can't. What about you, Jaime? . . . You can? Do you drive a truck at work? . . . You do. A big one or a small one? . . . A big truck. Where did you learn to drive a truck? . . . Your father taught you. And you, Xiao Lin, can you drive a truck? . . . You can. Do you drive a truck at work? . . . You did back in China. Did you enjoy it? . . . Not very much, huh? Yes, driving a truck is hard work.

UNIT 14: Where Does Carlos Work? (page 83)

Teaching note: Look at page 84 while presenting page 83, asking the questions that appear beside each picture. Ask each question about Carlos first, and then ask the same question of your students. The words and phrases that appear with the pictures are Carlos's answers to the questions, but they also serve as cues for the questions. During the presentation, and again before beginning the pairwork (Activity 3), have volunteers model the questions as the students look at the pictures.

Sample presentation, Picture 1: Where does Carlos work?

Today we're going to talk about what Carlos does at work and in his free time. First, where does he work [pointing to the answer]? . . . He works at Talbot Construction. What about you, Chau? Where do you work? . . . At Safeway. And you, Zhen? Where do you work? . . . At the Comfort Inn. Now, can *you* make the question? "Where . . . ?" That's right, Van. Anyone else want to make the question? . . . Good, Maria. Now, can you ask about *Carlos*? "Where . . . ?" Right. Where does he work?

UNIT 15: What's the Matter with Susan? (page 91)

Teaching note: You will ask students a question during the presentation that is not answered in the book: *Why* does this person have this problem? Students are to speculate freely.

Ask questions like the following to present the pictures:

- What's the problem with this person?
- How do you know he/she has a_____?
- Why does he/she have a _____? (free speculation)
- Do you ever get a _____?
- Why/When do you have a_____?
- What do you do when you have a_____ ?

The Pictures

1. a cold
2. cough
3. sore throat (throat hurts)
4. the flu/fever and chills
5. earache (ear hurts)
6. sick to her stomach
7. diarrhea
8. rash
9. toothache (tooth hurts)
10. cramps
11. dizzy
12. run-down

Sample presentation, Picture 1: She has a cold.

Take a look at these people. How do they look to you? . . . Yes, they're sick. Today we're going to talk about health problems. What's "health"? . . . Yes, it's our bodies, if we feel sick or healthy. Let's look at Susan. What's the matter with her? . . . She has a cold. How do you know Susan has a cold? . . . She's lying in bed . . . She looks miserable. And why do you think she got this cold? Any ideas? . . . Yes, maybe she went out without a coat . . . Or

maybe she went out in the rain. Could be. Do *you* ever get a cold? . . . You do, Elena? What do you do when you get a cold? . . . You rest in bed. What do other people do when they get a cold? . . . You drink tea? . . . You have chicken soup? . . .

UNIT 16: Is Carlos Going to Go to Work on Thursday? (page 99)

Teaching note: For each of the four story lines on page 99, ask:

- *what* is going to happen next Tuesday and Wednesday.
- *if* the depicted action is going to happen on Thursday. (This will be a matter of speculation.)

Use the expression *going to* (for future) in the presentation, but do not ask students to produce it until it is formally presented on page 101.

Ask questions like the following to present the pictures:

- What is he/she going to do next Tuesday/Wednesday?
- Do you think he/she's going to _____on Thursday?
- Why do you think he/she is(n't) going to_____ on Thursday?
- Have/Do you ever _____?
- When did you last_____?
- How often do you _____?

The Pictures

Carlos
Tuesday—check into the hospital
Wednesday—have an operation
Thursday—go to work?

Ken and Judy
Tuesday—call in sick
Wednesday—go skiing
Thursday—feel bad?

Susan
Tuesday—have a tooth pulled
Wednesday—stay home
Thursday—eat ice cream?

the cat
Tuesday—drink soda
Wednesday—eat a hamburger
Thursday—have a stomachache?

Sample presentation, Story line 1: Carlos's week

Today we're going to talk about what these people are going to do next week. What's Carlos going to do on Tuesday? Is he going to check into a hotel, or check into a hospital? . . . He's going to check into a hospital. When do you check into a hospital? . . . Yes, when you're sick. Does that mean you're going *into* or *leaving* the hospital? . . . It means you're going into it. What else do we check into? . . . Yes, we check into a hotel. Now, what's Carlos going to do on Wednesday? . . . He's going to have an operation. What does that mean? . . . Right. An operation is when they cut you open. Did anyone here ever have an operation? . . . You did, Pablo? Here, or in your country? . . . I see. I know, it's no fun. I had an operation three years ago myself. So, on Tuesday, Carlos is going to . . . check into the hospital. And on Wednesday he's going to . . . have an operation. Now, what do you think? Is he going to go to work on Thursday? . . . You say he isn't going to go, Joycelin? Why not? . . . Because he'll be resting at home. And you think he's going to go, Theo? . . . Oh, I see, if it's a small operation.

UNIT 17: When Is Ken Going to Move? (page 105)

Teaching note: This unit is atypical in that students will be producing statements just after you have presented the vocabulary, as in the sample presentation below. Allow several students to produce each of the statements and allow extra time for this presentation.

Ask these questions about Ken on Friday:

1. What's Ken going to do?
   (Move to a new apartment.)

2. Where's he going to move?
   (Around the corner [from his old place].)

3. What time is he going to move?
   (In the morning.)

Ask these questions about Ken on Saturday:

1. What's Ken going to do on Saturday?
   (Buy chairs for his new apartment.)

2. How many chairs is he going to buy?
   (Four.)

3. Who's he going shopping for the chairs with?
   (Judy.)

4. How's he going to take the chairs home?
   (In his car.)

Ask these questions about the kids on Friday:

1. What are the kids going to do on Friday?
   (See a movie.)

2. Where are they going to see the movie?
   (Downtown.)

3. Who are they going to go to the movie with?
   (Their parents.)

4. When are they going to see the movie?
   (At night.)

Ask these questions about the kids on Saturday:

1. What are the kids going to do on Saturday?
   (Ride a merry-go-round.)

2. Where are they going to ride the merry-go-round?
   (At the park.)

3. When are they going to go to the park?
   (In the afternoon.)

4. How are they going to get to the park?
   ([They're going to] walk.)

Ask these questions about the cat on Friday:

1. What's the cat going to do on Friday?
   (Play checkers.)

2. When's the cat going to play checkers?
   (All day.)

3. Who's the cat going to play with?
   (The parrot.)

4. Where are they going to play?
   (In the living room.)

Ask this question about the cat on Saturday:

1. What's the cat going to do on Saturday?
   (Nothing.)

Sample presentation, Picture 1: what Ken is going to do on Friday

Let's see what Ken's going to do next Friday. Is he going to paint his house, or is he going to move? . . . He's going to move. What does that mean? . . . Yes, it means change to a new house. Did any of you move recently? . . . You did, Kim? Where did you move to? . . . To Taylor Street. Now, where's Ken going to move to [pointing]? . . . Yes, he's going to move around the corner from his old apartment. So is he going to move *far* or *close* to his old place? . . . Close. Just around the corner. And *when* is he going to move [pointing]? . . . He's going to move in the morning. How do you know? . . . Yes, because the sun is going up. Now look at the picture and listen. [Slowly, pointing to individual parts of the picture:] On Friday morning, Ken's going to move to a new apartment around the corner. Who can say that? . . . Joon, you want to try? Go ahead . . .

UNIT 18: Will I Be Rich? (page 111)

Teaching note: Focus on the vocabulary during the presentation, using any appropriate structures to talk about it. Do not focus on the modal *will* until the questions and responses are formally presented on page 113.

Ask questions like the following to present the pictures:

- Do you want to＿＿＿＿＿?

- Why do(n't) you want to＿＿＿＿＿?

- Do you think you will＿＿＿＿＿?

- Why do(n't) you think you will＿＿＿＿＿?

- Do you know people who＿＿＿＿＿?

The Pictures

1. be rich
2. be famous
3. meet the president
4. get a raise
5. get a promotion
6. get a new job
7. go back to your country
8. travel around the world
9. go to the moon
10. have great-grandchildren
11. have white hair
12. ???

Sample presentation, Picture 1: be rich

Today I'm going to ask you some questions about the future. See this guy? He has a lot of . . . money. That means he's . . . rich. Now who here wants to be rich in the future? . . . Everyone does. No surprise. But tell me, Diego, why do you want to be rich? . . . Oh, so you can buy a new house. And you, Helen, why do you want to be rich? . . . Oh, to go back to your country. And Kevin, do you think you'll be rich? . . . You don't? How come? . . . Because it's hard to find a good job here. I understand. What about you, Teresa, do you think you'll be rich someday? . . . You do! . . . Oh, you have a good idea for a business. I wish you good luck!

UNIT 19: What Did Carlos Do on Monday? (page 117)

Teaching note: Use the past tense in your presentation, but do not ask students to produce it until it is formally introduced on page 118.

Ask questions like the following to present the pictures:

- What did (Carlos) do on (Tuesday)?
- Why did (he) _____? (free speculation)
- Do/Did you ever _____?
- How much (money) did you _____?
- When did you _____?
- Does your cat ever _____?

The Pictures

Carlos
Monday— opened a bank account
Tuesday— deposited money
Wednesday— shopped all day
Thursday— closed the bank account

Ken and Judy
Monday— borrowed money
Tuesday— traveled to Las Vegas
Wednesday— gambled all day
Thursday— returned the money

the cat
Monday— looked at mice
Tuesday— chased mice

Wednesday— cooked the mice
Thursday—didn't do anything

Sample presentation, Picture 1: open a bank account

Today we're going to talk about what these people did last week. What did Carlos do on Monday? . . . Well, did he open a *book*, or open a *bank account*? . . . He opened a bank account. What is a bank account? . . . Yes, it's when we keep our money in the bank. And what does it mean to *open* an account? . . . Yes, it means we start a new account. Did any of you open an account when you came here? . . . You did, Heng Li? When did you open your account? . . . Last year. Where? . . . At First National. Now, why do you think Carlos opened a new account? . . . Yes, maybe he just moved. Or? . . . Oh, Chen, what an idea! You think he wants to hide his money from his wife! Well, could be...

UNIT 20: Did you live near a post office in your country? (page 123)

Teaching note: Elicit short answers during the presentation, and, if necessary, help students with the responses "Yes, I did" and "No, I didn't."

Ask questions like the following to present the pictures:

- Did you _____ in your country?
- How often did you _____?
- What kind of _____ did you _____?
- Who did you _____ with?
- Where did you _____?
- Why didn't you _____?

The Pictures

1. live near a post office
2. pray at church/temple
3. watch movies
4. use the library
5. visit museums
6. shop at department stores
7. play sports
8. use trains
9. attend concerts
10. live in a big city
11. travel a lot
12. study English

Sample presentation, Pictures 1 and 2: live near a post office; attend church/temple

Today I'm going to ask you about things you did in your country. Ping, did you live near a post office in China? . . . You did. How far was it? . . . Oh, across the street. That *is* close! Did you live near a post office in Burma, Mei Lin? . . . You didn't. And you, Francisco? . . . You didn't either. Now, let's look at the next picture. What's this? . . . It's a church or a temple. What do people do at church or temple [demonstrating with hands]? . . . People pray. Are there many temples in China, Kim? . . .

There are? And in Vietnam? . . . Yes. What about in Guatemala? . . . Oh, mostly churches there. Did you pray at church in Guatemala, Juan? . . . You did. Who did you go to church with? . . . Your family. What about you, Mei Lin? Did you pray at temples in Burma? . . . You did. How often did you pray? . . . Every day. When do people usually pray in this country? . . . Yes, often on Sundays.

UNIT 21: Did You Go Shopping Last Weekend? (page 129)

Ask questions like the following to present the pictures:

- Did you _____ last weekend?
- Where did you _____?
- Who did you _____ with?
- How did you get there?
- When was the last time you _____?
- Why didn't you _____?

The Pictures

1. go shopping
2. see friends
3. eat out
4. get a haircut
5. have fun
6. come home late
7. meet somebody new
8. sleep late
9. leave the city
10. write a letter
11. speak English
12. tell a lie

Sample presentation, Picture 1: go shopping

Today we're going to talk about things we did last weekend. Noe, did you go shopping last weekend? . . . You didn't. What about you, Silvia, did you go shopping last weekend? . . . Yes, you did. And where did you go shopping? . . . In Chinatown. Who did you go with? . . . Your mother. And you, Mohammed? Did you go shopping? . . . You did. How did you get to the store? . . . You drove. OK, let's go to the next picture. Jin Tong, did you see your friends last weekend? . . .

UNIT 22: What Happened to Judy? (page 135)

Teaching note: Look at pages 136 and 137 while presenting page 135. For each picture, ask:

- What happened to this person?
- What should somebody do to help?

The sentences on pages 136 and 137 comprise the target vocabulary for the presentation (i.e., answers to the above two questions), but students should be encouraged to suggest other ways to describe (or respond to) the problem.

Sample presentation, Picture 1: a dog bite

Today we're going to talk about accidents and emergencies. What are accidents? . . . Yes, like a car accident. What else? . . . Yes, when someone falls down. We see several accidents in these pictures. And what's an emergency? . . . Yes, something very bad—a big problem. And we need . . . ? Yes, we need help fast. Look at the first picture. What happened to Judy? . . . Yes, a dog bit her. *Bit* is the past tense of *bite*. And what does *bite* mean? Show me . . . Right, that's what *bite* is. So this dog bit Judy, and what's happening to her hand? . . . Yes, it's bleeding. Can you see [pointing to blood]? When you're bleeding, what color is it? . . . Yes, it's red. Which hand of Judy's is bleeding? . . . Her right hand. So now that a dog bit Judy and her hand is bleeding, what should we do? . . . Yes, we can call 911. What else should we do? . . . Yes, we should wash her hand . . . What else? . . . That's called a bandage, Minh. We should put a bandage on her hand. Do you know what a bandage is? Here, let me draw one on the chalkboard for you. Where do you buy bandages? . . . At the drugstore. Do you keep bandages in your house? . . . Where? . . . You keep bandages in the bathroom. Me too. So, we'll wash her hand, put on a bandage, and call 911. Anything else? What about the dog? Is it OK if the dog goes away? . . . No. How come? . . . Yes, it can make Judy very sick. So what should we do? . . . Yes, we should watch the dog until the police come.

UNIT 23: Where did Carlos have his checkup? (page 143)

Teaching note: This unit is atypical in that students will be producing statements just after you have presented the vocabulary, as in the sample presentation below. Allow several students to produce each of the statements and allow extra time for this presentation.

Ask these questions about Carlos on Friday:

1. What did Carlos do on Friday?
   (He had a checkup.)
2. Where did he have the checkup?
   (At the clinic.)
3. When did he have the checkup?
   (At noon.)
4. How did he get to the clinic?
   (By bus.)

Ask these questions about Carlos on Saturday:

1. What did Carlos do on Saturday?
   (He went jogging.)
2. Where did he go jogging?
   (In the park.)
3. What time did he go jogging?
   (In the morning.)
4. How far did he run?
   (Five miles.)

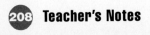

Ask these questions about Judy on Friday:

1. What did Judy do on Friday?
   (She played tennis.)

2. Who did she play tennis with?
   (With Ken.)

3. When did they play tennis?
   (After work.)

4. How did they get to the park?
   (They walked.)

Ask these questions about Judy on Saturday:

1. What did Judy do on Saturday?
   (She watched TV.)

2. Where did she watch TV?
   (At home.)

3. Who did she watch TV with?
   (Her dog.)

4. Why did she watch TV?
   (Because her feet were sore.)

Ask these questions about the parrot on Friday:

1. What did the parrot do on Friday?
   (He talked all day.)

2. Who did he talk to?
   (The cat.)

3. How many languages did he speak?
   (Three.)

Ask these questions about the parrot on Saturday:

1. What did the parrot do on Saturday?
   (He drank tea.)

2. What kind of tea did he drink?
   (Lemon and honey tea.)

3. How many cups did he drink?
   (Seven.)

4. Why did he drink so much tea?
   (Because he had a sore throat.)

Sample presentation, Picture 1: Carlos having a checkup

Today we're going to talk about what these people did last Friday and Saturday. What did Carlos do on Friday? . . . Yes, he had a checkup. What's a checkup? . . . Yes, when we see the doctor. Because we're sick? . . . No. We have a checkup to make sure everything's OK. Does Carlos's doctor look happy? . . . No, he doesn't. Why not, do you think? . . . Yes, Carlos is too fat. What do you think the doctor told Carlos? . . . Yes, maybe to get some exercise. Now, where did Carlos go for his checkup [pointing]? . . . He went to the clinic. Do you remember what a clinic is? . . . Yes, a doctor's office. When did Carlos have his checkup [pointing]? . . . At noon. And how did he get to the clinic [pointing]? . . . He took the bus.

UNIT 24: Yesterday, Today, and Tomorrow (page 151)

Teaching note: During the presentation, the focus should be on the new vocabulary. During the conversation practice (Activity 4), more attention can be given to proper tense selection.

Ask questions like the following to present the pictures:

- What did (the Satos) do (two days ago)?
- What are (they) doing right now?
- What are they going to do tomorrow?
- Why is he/she feeling _____?
- Have/Do you ever _____?
- When did/do you _____?

The Pictures

the Satos
2 days ago—made reservations
yesterday—bought plane tickets
right now—flying to Hawaii
tomorrow—lie in the sun

Judy
2 days ago—packed her suitcase
yesterday—kissed Ken goodbye
right now—feeling lonely
tomorrow—call Ken

Carlos
2 days ago—ate ice cream
yesterday—weighed himself
right now—feeling bad
tomorrow—go on a diet

Sample presentation, Picture 1: the Satos making reservations

Let's see what's happening with our friends this week. You see, the Satos are taking a trip. But what did they do two days ago? Did they make hamburgers, or make reservations? . . . They made reservations. What does that mean? . . . Yes, you make reservations for your plane ticket. You call the airlines, and what do you tell them? . . . The day . . . and time . . . and place you're going. Also, they made reservations for what [pointing]? . . . Yes, they made reservations for their hotel. What do you say when you make hotel reservations? . . . Yes, what day you're going, and . . . how many people, and . . . how many nights you're staying. So the Satos made plane and hotel reservations two days ago.

UNIT 25: What Should I Do Next? (page 157)

Teaching note: Look at page 158 while presenting page 157, and introduce the language in the captions by asking about what is happening in each picture. Then, for each picture, ask the students for instructions—as though they were your supervisor at work—to elicit the language you have introduced. (See sample presentation below.) Students will not be formally introduced to—or produce—questions with *should* until the conversation practice (page 159).

Introduce each picture by asking:

• What is the worker *doing*?
• What is he/she *using* to do the job?
• *How many* is he/she _____ing?
• *What color* is he/she using? (Pictures 3 and 4 only)

Then tell the students they are your supervisor and ask, for each picture:

• What should I *do* next?
• What should I *use* to_____?
• *How many* should I _____?
• *What color*_____should I use? (Pictures 3 and 4 only)

Sample presentation for page 157, Picture 1: peeling apples

Today we're going to talk again about things people do at work. What's happening in this picture? . . . Is the person *eating* apples or *peeling* apples? . . . Yes, he's peeling apples. What else do we peel? . . . Yes, we peel bananas, and . . . oranges, and . . . sometimes we peel potatoes. Now, what's this guy using to peel the apples [pointing]? . . . He's using a knife. And how many apples is he peeling? . . . Two pounds. Now, let's practice. I'm the worker and you're my supervisor. OK? Tell me, boss, what should I do next [pointing]? . . . OK. And what should I use to peel them? . . . All right. And how many should I peel? Got it! Now, class, let's look at the next picture . . .

Presenting page 160

(1) Present all six pictures by introducing the language at the bottom of page 160 in the same way you introduced the language on page 158. (Each sentence corresponds to the picture with the same number.) (2) Tell your students again that they are your supervisor and, pointing to the pictures one by one, ask, "What should I do now, boss?" thus eliciting the instructions you have just introduced. This time, however, ask a clarification question (suggested clearly by each picture) in response to each instruction from the students:

Instruction (from students)	Your clarification question
1. Wipe the cabinet.	You mean the inside or the outside?
2. Change the light bulb.	You mean the left one or the right one?
3. Sweep the restroom.	You mean the men's room or the women's room?
4. Put this in the drawer.	You mean the top one or the bottom one?
5. Empty the wastebasket.	You mean the tall one or the short one?
6. Weigh the package.	You mean the big one or the small one?

(Your "supervisors" can answer your clarification questions as they wish.)

Before students begin conversation practice, point out and model the intonation pattern indicated by the arrows in the box.

UNIT 26: You Should Never Do That! (page 163)

Teaching note: Look at page 164 while presenting page 163, and introduce the language by asking:

• What's the problem?
• Why isn't this safe?

Clarify the meanings of *should never, should always,* and *might* as you introduce them. Reinforce the new vocabulary by relating it to your students' lives, as in the sample presentation below.

Sample presentation, Picture 1: bending over to pick up something heavy

Today we're going to talk about safety on the job. What's "safety"? . . . Yes, it means you are safe. Does that mean you have an accident? . . . No. Safety means you don't have accidents. Look at this person. What's he doing? . . . Yes, he's picking something up. Is it light or heavy? . . . It's heavy. And how is he doing that [demonstrating]? . . . He's bending over. For example, when do we bend over? . . . When we drop something or . . . when we tie our shoes. Is it a good idea to bend over when we pick up something heavy? . . . No, it isn't. We *should never* bend over to pick up something heavy. What do I mean, "should never"? . . . Yes, it means it's not a good idea. And why shouldn't we bend over to pick up heavy things? Because we might . . . yes, we might hurt our back. What do I mean, "might"? . . . Yes, "maybe." If we pick up something this way, maybe we'll hurt our back.

UNIT 27: Is Your Hometown Rainy? (page 169)

Teaching note: Before beginning the presentation, write the word *compare* and the ending *-er* on the chalkboard, and tell students that we use *-er* to compare. Establish the meaning of *compare* with a few simple examples: Have two students stand, and say, "Tran is taller"; point to a young student and say, "I am older," and so forth. Elicit only short answers during the presentation; students will not be asked to produce comparative statements or questions until these are introduced on pages 171 and 172.

Ask questions like the following to present the pictures on page 169:

• Do you like _____cities?
• Do you know a city/country that's very_____?
• Is your hometown_____?
• Is our city_____?
• Which is _____er, your hometown or our city? (A little_____er or a lot _____er?)

The Pictures

1. rainy	7. quiet
2. hilly	8. clean
3. cold	9. safe
4. windy	10. busy
5. big	11. friendly
6. old	12. cheap

Sample presentation for page 169, Picture 1: rainy

Today we're going to talk about your hometown and our city. Do you like rainy cities [pointing to the picture]? . . . You don't, Javier? How come? . . . Oh, you always have to carry your umbrella in rainy places . . . And sometimes your shoes get wet when it's rainy. Do you know a place that's very rainy? . . . Hong Kong is rainy in June . . . and Seattle is rainy. What about your hometown, Ali? Is it rainy there? . . . Not very rainy. What about you, Chau? Which is rainier, your hometown or our city? . . . Your hometown is rainier. Is it a little rainier or a lot rainier? . . . Oh, it's a lot rainier.

Presenting page 173

Refer to the cues at the bottom of the page during your presentation. For each pair of pictures, ask:

• Which do you like better/more, _____ ing or _____ ing?

• Why do you like _____ ing more?

Before students begin conversation practice, point out and model the intonation pattern indicated by the arrows in the box.

UNIT 28: Is Your Hometown Crowded? (page 175)

Teaching note: Before beginning the presentation, tell students that we sometimes use *more* to compare. (The rule

for using *-er* or *more* will be formally presented on page 177.) Elicit short answers during the presentation.

Ask questions like the following to present the pictures:

• Do you like _____ cities?

• Do you know a city/country that's very _____ ?

• Is your hometown _____ ?

• Is our city _____ ?

• Which is more _____ , your hometown or our city? (A lot more _____ or a little more _____ ?)

The Pictures

1. crowded
2. beautiful
3. modern
4. expensive
5. dangerous
6. scenic
7. famous
8. interesting
9. fun

Sample presentation, Picture 1: crowded

Today we're going to talk some more about your hometown and our city. Do you like cities that are crowded [pointing to the picture]? . . . Looks like you don't. What does it mean when a city is crowded? . . . Yes, it means a lot of people close together. For example, where is it crowded in our city? . . . It's crowded on the buses. Where else? . . . It's crowded in Chinatown. What about your hometown, Sandra? Is it very crowded? . . . It isn't. Abdullah, which is more crowded, your hometown or our city? . . . Your hometown. Well, is it a lot more crowded or just a little more crowded? . . . Oh, it's a lot more crowded.